NEXT NEW YORK

40 IDEAS FOR THE FUTURE OF THE BUILT ENVIRONMENT
A PROJECT OF THE FORUM FOR URBAN DESIGN

Next New York: 40 Ideas for the Future of the Built Environment
© 2013 The Forum for Urban Design

Edited by Christopher Beardsley and Daniel McPhee

Contributors: Maria Aiolova, Laurie Beckelman, Vicki Been, Lance Jay Brown, Donald Capoccia, Nette Compton, Jay Cross, Peter Derrick, Susannah Drake, Jacob Dugopolski, Kathleen Dunn, Elliot Felix, Ben Fried, Alexander Garvin, David Giles, Mark Ginsberg, Will Goodman, MaryAnne Gilmartin, Gregory Haley, Fred Harris, Naomi Hersson-Ringskog, Mitchell Joachim, Thomas Jost, Paul Katz, Carol Lamberg, Deborah Marton, Robert Quinlan, Nina Rappaport, Chris Reed, Sam Schwartz, Ronald Shiffman, Steven Spinola, Marilyn Jordan Taylor, Mark Thomann, Claire Weisz, Andrew Whalley, Paul Steely White, Madelyn Wils, Robert Yaro, Mark Yoes

Design: Rachelle Vagy, Emily DePietro
Graphic Support: Ellis Calvin, Hanson Cheng
Editorial Support: James Dashiell Henley, Christiana Whitcomb, Logan Woodruff
Printing and Binding: Village Print

The ideas expressed are those of the contributors and do not reflect the opinions of the Forum for Urban Design. Some images and texts have been modified for clarity by the editors of this publication. All attempts have been made to maintain the core concepts of each project as intended by the individual authors.

The Forum for Urban Design
Long Island City, New York
www.ffud.org

All rights reserved. No part of this book may be reproduced in any form or by any means without permission in writing from the publisher, except brief passages for review purposes.

ISBN: 978-0-9791869-2-9
Library of Congress Control Number: 2013944711

Printed in the United States of America

♻ This book was printed on Cougar Domtar using 100% post-consumer recycled materials

THE FORUM FOR URBAN DESIGN

The Forum For Urban Design convenes the world's preeminent leaders in architecture, urban planning, design and development—as well as professionals in government, education and journalism whose work intersects with the built environment—to discuss and debate the defining issues that face our cities. The Forum, based in New York City, engages its fellows through programs and publications that promote awareness of contemporary urban design's best practices and greatest challenges.

Board of Directors:
Daniel Rose, Chair
Alexander Garvin, President
Deborah Berke, Vice President
James Corner, Vice President
Paul Katz, Treasurer
Meredith J. Kane, Secretary
Marilyn Jordan Taylor, Immediate Past President
Daniel Brodsky
Timur Galen
Paul Goldberger
Hugh Hardy
David Haskell
Robert Yaro

Christopher Beardsley, Executive Director
Daniel McPhee, Deputy Director

TABLE OF CONTENTS

INTRODUCTION	8
NOTE FROM OUR PARTNERS	10
PARTICIPANTS	12

INVESTMENTS IN THE PUBLIC REALM

ONE REGIONAL RAIL SYSTEM 16
Peter Derrick

SKY AND WATER LINKS 18
Claire Weisz, Mark Yoes, and Jacob Dugopolski

THE NEW YORK TRIBORO OVERGROUND 20
Robert Yaro

LIGHT RAIL FOR THE BROOKLYN-QUEENS 22
WATERFRONT
Alexander Garvin

EXTEND THE 7 LINE TO SECAUCUS 24
Jay Cross

REIMAGINE PENN STATION 26
Marilyn Jordan Taylor

BUILDING A REGIONAL IDENTITY 28
CONVERSATION: NEXT NEW YORK: AIR + RAIL

EXPRESS CONNECTIONS TO THE 32
REGION'S AIRPORTS
Grimshaw Architects: Andrew Whalley and Gregory Haley

ONE-SEAT RIDE TO LAGUARDIA 34
Alexander Garvin

SUPERCHARGED TRANSIT CORRIDORS 36
Claire Weisz, Mark Yoes, and Jacob Dugopolski

BUILD A BUS RAPID TRANSIT NETWORK 38
Ben Fried

BIKE SUPERHIGHWAYS 40
Paul Steely White

STREETS FOR THE TWENTY-FIRST CENTURY 42
CONVERSATION: NEXT NEW YORK: ROADS + BRIDGES

ACTIVATE THE QUEENSWAY 46
Laurie Beckelman

CAP THE BROOKLYN-QUEENS EXPRESSWAY 48
Susannah Drake

LET THE WATER IN 50
Chris Reed

RIPARIAN BUFFERS ALONG THE WATERFRONT 52
Maria Aiolova and Mitchell Joachim

FLOATING ISLANDS 54
Mark Thomann

ATTRACTING DIVERSITY IN AN AFFLUENT CITY 56
CONVERSATION: NEXT NEW YORK: ARTS + CULTURE

EMBRACE MODULAR HOUSING 60
MaryAnne Gilmartin

RE-SKIN PUBLIC HOUSING 62
Fred Harris

AFFORDABLE HOUSING FOR YOUNG NEW 64
YORKERS
Robert Quinlan

INVIGORATE OUR PUBLIC LIBRARIES 65
David Giles

IMPROVEMENTS TO CITY OPERATIONS

THE NYC DEPARTMENT OF FOOD — 68
Tom Jost

RESTORE THE CAPITAL BUDGET TO CITY PLANNING — 70
Ronald Shiffman

REFORM THE LANDMARKS PRESERVATION COMMISSION — 71
Steven Spinola

FOUR FORMULAS FOR SENSIBLE DENSITY — 72
Mark Ginsberg

STREAMLINE AFFORDABLE HOUSING EXEMPTIONS — 74
Kathleen Dunn

MAKE ROOM FOR MIDDLE-INCOME HOUSING — 76
Steven Spinola

REWRITE THE REQUEST FOR PROPOSALS — 77
Carol Lamberg

A NEW GENERATION OF CONSTRUCTION TRADE WORKERS — 78
Donald Capoccia

EMPOWER SHARED RESOURCE MODELS — 79
Elliot Felix

REDUCING THE COST OF NEW HOUSING — 80
CONVERSATION: NEXT NEW YORK: HOUSING

THE CZAR OF PUBLIC SPACE — 84
Lance Jay Brown

FOSTER HEALTHY, INTEGRATED COMMUNITIES — 85
Ronald Shiffman

DYNAMIC ZONING — 86
Jonathan Rose Companies: Will Goodman

VERTICAL URBAN FACTORIES — 88
Nina Rappaport

LEVEL THE TOLLS — 90
Sam Schwartz

EXPAND LANDMARKS' ABILITY TO TRANSFER AIR RIGHTS — 92
Vicki Been

ZONING TO FOSTER VIBRANT COMMUNITIES — 94
CONVERSATION: NEXT NEW YORK: ZONING + DEVELOPMENT

LEVERAGE OUR VACANT SPACES — 98
Naomi Hersson-Ringskog

5,000 GREENSTREETS — 99
Nette Compton

TRANSFER DEVELOPMENT RIGHTS TO UPLAND AREAS — 100
Susannah Drake

SOCIAL IMPACT INVESTMENT IN PARKS + OPEN SPACES — 102
Deborah Marton

CAPTURE THE VALUE OF PARKS + PUBLIC SPACE — 104
Madelyn Wils

THE VALUE OF THE PUBLIC REALM — 106
CONVERSATION: NEXT NEW YORK: PARKS + OPEN SPACES

INTRODUCTION

As New Yorkers consider the coming election, there is an opportunity to assess the most critical issues facing the city. How will we contend with the city's swelling population? How will we rebuild our aging infrastructure and housing stock? And how will we protect our waterfront from the rising tide? The Forum for Urban Design has responded to that opportunity by inviting leading experts to address those challenges.

During the spring of 2013, we called upon the Fellows of the Forum—a diverse group of real estate developers, architects, urban designers, and public officials—to make proposals for the next mayor to consider. Over a series of seven breakfasts, we considered proposals to improve housing, open space, transportation, zoning, and arts and culture. The rules were simple: proposals had to be bold and no longer than five minutes. Forty courageous proposals emerged for reimagined infrastructure, reformed government, and an animated public realm.

This book presents the individual proposals made by our Fellows and invited experts. These proposals do not constitute a blueprint or a cohesive vision for the next administration, but they do present important ideas. Our aim in presenting them is to open a debate about how to create a more livable, competitive, and sustainable city.

We have divided this collection into two groups. The first segment presents key investments in the public realm, from rebuilt railways to supercharged streetscapes. The second contains essential improvements to city operations, from new zoning to reformed city agencies.

Some of the proposals offer highly pragmatic suggestions, while others inspire us with their visionary approaches. Some draw on the success of cities like London, Paris or Chicago, while others address the unique challenges facing New York. Some propose new solutions to age-old problems, like connections to LaGuardia Airport, retrofitting public housing, or extending the 7 Line.

Many of the proposals even confront the same spaces: Queens Boulevard, 21st Avenue, and Kent Avenue, for instance. These are sites in need of retrofits and re-imagination. Our contributors may have proposed solutions that are at odds with one another, so we hope this publication will spark a spirited debate about the future of the public realm.

After our contributors had the opportunity to pitch their ideas, we opened the floor for debate. Our fellows and invited experts were welcome to praise or critique the proposals, or even offer spontaneous suggestions of their own. Scattered throughout this book are fragments of six of our conversations.

Please, continue to share your ideas for the Next New York with us, no matter how eccentric or exact. Let's build an even better city.

Alexander Garvin
President, Board of Directors
Forum for Urban Design

NOTE FROM OUR PARTNERS

The Bloomberg administration is among the most successful in the history of our city in large part because it has focused on the transformative power of urban design to improve our quality of life and strengthen our economy. Mayor Bloomberg's emphasis on the creation of public space alone has yielded outstanding results, and his vision will likely be continued for many years to come.

The Next New York conversations were both an opportunity to reflect on our city and a reflection of the city itself. A diverse group of talented and busy people gathered to volunteer their ideas for the good of the city. One could only be impressed with how the contributors had considered the challenges and responded with new ideas, many of which could indeed by implemented. Several were extremely simple, which is, of course, the basis of great design.

The ideas—some entirely new, others more familiar—suggest an emerging consensus on planning directions for the coming years, on topics ranging from such small-scale proposals as planting individual street corners to such major initiatives as new transit corridors.

Some of the most encouraging proposals suggest possible innovations in technology— innovations fueled, in part, by the advancements we have made in urban design and planning. Great cities like New York capitalize on this reciprocal relationship between innovation and design.

As I reflect on the Next New York, I consider Hudson Yards, where so many of the Bloomberg administration's signature projects converge, from the High Line, to Hudson River Park, to the 7 Line extension. Such initiatives are a testament to the vision of New York. As we continue to adapt our city to the 21st century, I can only hope we meet the coming challenges with such vision.

Paul Katz
Principal, Kohn Pedersen Fox
Director, Forum for Urban Design

SPECIAL THANKS

The Next New York series and publication would not have been possible without the gracious support of many people.

First, we thank the over forty contributors who generously shared their visionary ideas with us over the last several months.

We sincerely thank the Board of Directors of the Forum for Urban Design for their guidance as we developed this series. In particular, thank you to Daniel Rose, Alexander Garvin, and Marilyn Taylor for shaping this project, and to Daniel Brodsky, Timur Galen, Hugh Hardy, Meredith Kane, and Robert Yaro, who kindled spirited debates week after week.

We are extremely grateful to Paul Katz and our colleagues at Kohn Pedersen Fox, who made this project possible. Special thanks to Krissie Nuckols and Gretchen Krueger for organizing several outstanding breakfasts, Rachelle Vagy for designing this book, and Hanson Cheng for assisting with our graphics.

Thank you also to John Alschuler and HR&A Advisors for their support in presenting our project to the greater public.

Thanks to Forum interns Ellis, Logan, Christiana, and Dash for their patience and persistence as we compiled this book.

And finally, thank you to the Fellows of the Forum for Urban Design. We are constantly inspired by your creative thinking and your readiness to build better cities.

Christopher Beardsley and
Daniel McPhee
Forum for Urban Design

PARTICIPANTS

Fatemeh Abbas Zadeh
Maria Aiolova, contributor
Richard Anderson
Brett Appel
Tobias Armborst
Robert Balder
Caroline Bauer
Ryan Baxter
Christopher Beardsley
Laurie Beckelman, contributor
Carmi Bee
Vicki Been, contributor
Rick Bell
Richard Bender
Adrian Benepe
Deborah Berke
Eugenie Birch
Frederick Bland
Bethany Bowyer
David Bragdon
Pippa Brashear
Daniel Brodsky
Lance Jay Brown, contributor
Charles Burton
Jeff Byles
Ellis Calvin
Andrew Cantor
Sara Caples
Donald Capoccia, contributor
Susan Chin
Ruth Cole
Nette Compton, contributor
Mihnea Constantinescu
Jay Cross, contributor
David Cunningham
Ali Davis
Peter Derrick, contributor
Ben Dodd
Nicole Dooskin

Susannah Drake, contributor
Jacob Dugopolski, contributor
Kathleen Dunn, contributor
Joel Ettinger
Ariel Fausto
Elliot Felix, contributor
Wendy Feuer
Connie Fishman
Lukas Fitze
Rosamond Fletcher
Adam Forman
Ben Fried, contributor
Timur Galen
Alex Garvin, contributor
Ray Gastil
Jean Marie Gath
Rosalie Genevro
Sarah Gerber
David Giles, contributor
MaryAnne Gilmartin, contributor
Mark Ginsberg, contributor
Paul Goldberger
Will Goodman, contributor
Wylie Goodman
Beth Greenberg
Nick Griffin
Anne Guiney
George Haikalis
Gregory Haley, contributor
Frances Halsband
Abby Hamlin
Hugh Hardy
Fred Harris, contributor
Frank Hebbert
David Hecht
Dash Henley
Naomi Hersson-Ringskog, contributor
John Hill
Matthias Hollwich

Brian Hong
William Hubbard
Arthur Imperatore, Jr.
Bjarke Ingels
Charles Ippolito
Jia Jia
Mitchell Joachim, contributor
Patra Jongjiritat
Thomas Jost, contributor
Meredith Kane
Paul Katz
Jesse Keenan
Penny King
Carol Lamberg, contributor
Henry Lanier
Chuck Laven
Barbara Leeds
Jill Lerner
Theodore Liebman
Nina Liebman
James Lima
Greg Lindsay
Paimaan Lodhi
Bill Louie
Susan Lowance
Andrew Lynn
Kevin Maddox
Erica Maganti
Raju Mann
Deborah Marton, contributor
Rachel May
Cathleen McGuigan
Daniel McPhee
Bhushan Mondkar
Anthony Mosellie
Robert Paley
Barbara Paley
Mehul Patel
Jennifer Pehr

Thomas Petersen
Lee Pomeroy
Robert Quinlan, contributor
Michael Rapfogel
Nina Rappaport, contributor
Laura Raskin
Chris Reed, contributor
Anne Rieselbach
Ronnette Riley
Evan Rose
Lauren Rose
Daniel Rose
Richard Rubens
Aubrey Rutter
William Ryall
Michael Samuelian
James Sanders
Brian Schwagerl
Sam Schwartz, contributor
David Scobey
Zim Seferi
Ronald Shiffman, contributor
Daria Siegel
Lloyd Sigal
Gabriel Silberblatt
Susanna Sirefman
Michael Slattery
Michael Sorkin
Steven Spinola, contributor
Byron Stigge
Jeremiah Stoldt
Mark Strauss
Margaret Sullivan
Marilyn Taylor, contributor
Mark Thomann, contributor
Aaron Vaden-Youmans
David Vanderhoff
Ian Veidenheimer
Julia Vitullo-Martin

James von Klemperer
Andrew Wade
Roxanne Warren
Claire Weisz, contributor
Andrew Whalley, contributor
William Wheeler
Paul Steely White, contributor
Barbara Wilks
Mark Willis
Carol Willis
Madelyn Wils, contributor
Logan Woodruff
Robert Yaro, contributor
Mark Yoes, contributor

INVEST IN THE PUBLIC REALM

Is New York City adequately investing in the built environment for the benefit of future generations? What are the greatest opportunities for new public transit, open spaces, housing retrofits, or complete streets? How can we leverage existing infrastructure for new public purposes?

The following ideas are a collection of proposals for investment in the public realm. The views expressed are those of the contributors and do not reflect the opinions of the Forum for Urban Design.

ONE REGIONAL RAIL SYSTEM
Peter Derrick

We need a real regional rail system. All three commuter rail systems—Metro North, Long Island Rail Road, and New Jersey Transit—currently operate as separate entities.

There are three requirements for creating a truly regional rail system. The first is to allow through-running at Penn Station to allow New Jersey trains to travel through the city to Long Island and northern suburbs. Just like the subway system, trains would travel through Manhattan and terminate in the suburbs. Imagine if riders could travel from Coop City in the Bronx to Meadowlands Stadium, or from Princeton to New Haven, or from Flushing to New Jersey. Or if Long Island Railroad and Metro North trains could travel to New Jersey.

The second strategy is to connect new destinations by deep connections. Penn Station could be connected to Grand Central so all the train systems could pass through the city's main transit hubs. One could also build new tunnels from Atlantic Terminal in Brooklyn to Manhattan, or between the Queens rail network to JFK Airport.

Finally, you could build major rail stations in the outskirts of the city. This is a strategy similar to what Paris has done since the 1960s, where they connected rail stations by deep tunnels that serve almost 800 million riders a year.

The benefits are obvious. You free up capacity at Penn Station. You increase regional rail ridership with better connections to the suburbs, outer boroughs, and the airports. You provide a base for development along suburban nodes like Hicksville or Ronkonkoma. And you provide commuters with greater ease of service, with one common ticket and one information nexus.

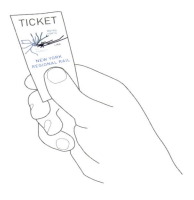

Peter Derrick is currently a Visiting Scholar at the Rudin Center for Transportation Policy and Management at the Robert F. Wagner Graduate School of Public Service at New York University.

SKY AND WATER LINKS

Claire Weisz, Mark Yoes + Jacob Dugopolski

Imagine new uninterrupted connections across the river, linking major destinations across the five boroughs.

First, we could extend the Roosevelt Island tram in both directions, creating a new link from Queens Plaza to Central Park. The tram could be a high-visibility attraction, steering tourists from Central Park to the museums and galleries of Long Island City. And it would serve commuters as an above-grade transit option with a fantastic view that links Queens Plaza with Midtown Manhattan or the new Roosevelt Island campus and innovation hub.

The East River Ferry could also be expanded to bridge neighborhoods directly across the river from one another. Paired with new bikeways and express bus routes along the waterfront, the ferry would offer a quicker transportation alternative to existing multi-stop bus and subway routes. The ferry should create new access points at Roosevelt Island; Pier 35, Houston Street, and Stuyvesant Cove in Manhattan; and Jay Street and the Brooklyn Navy Yard in Brooklyn.

Finally, we could invest in new bridges to unite our waterfront greenways. We could link Governors Island to Red Hook, Greenpoint and Long Island City along Manhattan Avenue, Harlem and Yankee Stadium along W. 153rd Street, Hunts Point and Soundview along Lafayette Avenue, and Gowanus and Red Hook along Centre Street.

Claire Weisz and Mark Yoes are Founding Principals of WXY Architecture + Urban Design, a New York-based firm focused on social and environmental transformation of the public realm at multiple scales. Jacob Dugopolski is an Architectural Designer and Project Manager with WXY.

THE NEW YORK TRIBORO OVERGROUND
Robert Yaro

The New York Triboro Overground is a regional express rail for the outer boroughs. The Overground would utilize the railbed of the existing New York Connecting Railroad, which carries limited freight traffic and connects Port Morris in the Bronx through Queens with Bay Ridge in Brooklyn. The Connecting Railroad has a four-track right-of-way over much of its length, and carries Amtrak trains over a portion of the right of way.

The Overground could be put into use relatively quickly, in phases, and starting with diesel self-propelled trains. By reviving this train line, we could connect virtually every subway line in the city except for those that run exclusively in Manhattan and provide an inter-borough alternative mobility system.

The Overground is inspired by the work that London did to prepare for the Olympics, where they pieced together under utilized freight lines and surface rights-of-way to create a loop around London and integrated them with the underground and bus system.

This is not the only answer to the mobility needs of the boroughs, but it would certainly provide alternate means of access between the boroughs and into Manhattan.

———

Let's see what we can do to enhance the limited freight traffic there. There are some areas that we could actually ride it, but it's also important to maintain some semblance of freight service and extend that to Long Island.
– David Bragdon

Robert D. Yaro is the President of the Regional Plan Association, the nation's oldest independent metropolitan policy, research, and advocacy group. He is also Professor of Practice at the University of Pennsylvania.

LIGHT RAIL FOR THE BROOKLYN-QUEENS WATERFRONT
Alexander Garvin

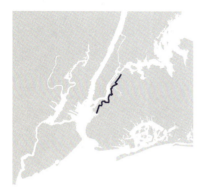

Some of the greatest opportunities for new housing and development within a stone's throw of Manhattan line the East River in Astoria and Long Island City. By creating a new light rail line in those neighborhoods, we could create an enormous opportunity for new investment.

Astoria is currently served by an elevated rail line that runs along 31st Street one mile east of the East River. I propose situating a new light rail line along 21st Street, the widest thoroughfare before reaching Vernon Boulevard. A first phase would connect Astoria with the F subway stop at 21st Street and Queens Plaza. A second phase could extend the rail line across Newtown Creek and along the Brooklyn waterfront to terminate in Red Hook.

The capital cost of the new light rail line could be financed from the tax increment generated by new and renovated housing created on underutilized properties within walking distance of the new light rail line.

Alexander Garvin is President and CEO of AGA Public Realm Strategists, a planning and design firm specializing in the public realm. He is Adjunct Professor of Urban Planning and Management at Yale University. He currently serves as the President of the Forum for Urban Design.

EXISTING

PROPOSED

EXTEND THE 7 LINE TO SECAUCUS
Jay Cross

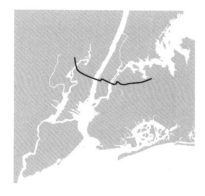

Hudson Yards lies at the crossroads of what I call the "High Culture Corridor" and the "Popular Culture Corridor." The "High Culture Corridor" extends from the new Whitney on Gansevoort along the High Line to the future Culture Shed at Hudson Yards. It is a lively area populated with galleries, restaurants, tourists and parks. The "Popular Culture Corridor" falls largely along the 7 Subway Line, linking the stadiums in Flushing, the arts communities of Long Island City, the theaters of 42nd Street, and Hudson Yards, but there is still incredible untapped potential here.

Let's push the extension of the 7-Line to Secaucus and bring the subway to New Jersey. The possibilities are extraordinary. We could host the Super Bowl at Meadowlands but its kick-off party in the middle of Manhattan. We could make Long Island City into a regional destination by promoting its art galleries and museums. We could draw new numbers to Flushing Meadows-Corona Park. And Hudson Yards could serve as a booming new cultural heart for the city.

Jay Cross is President of Related Hudson Yards, where he is leading the development efforts of the 26-acre Hudson Yards site on the west side of New York City.

REIMAGINE PENN STATION
Marilyn Jordan Taylor

Marilyn Jordan Taylor, FAIA, is the Dean and Paley Professor at the University of Pennsylvania School of Design. She is recognized worldwide as a thought leader in urban design, infrastructure, architecture and city building. See the PennDesign website to learn more about the work of Penn students in advancing region-shaping infrastructure and high-speed rail.

For fifty years, New Yorkers moved through one of the world's great urban gateways. Then, more than fifty years ago, victim to an age of decreased rail ridership, the station moved into the basement. Every day more than half a million people pour through the crowded, confusing corridors to platforms too narrow to handle passenger demand. It almost seems as if they—and we—have come to accept that it can never get better.

Pennsylvania Station must grow its capacity to serve 110 million passengers entering New York City annually—more than the three major metro airports combined. A new Penn Station will renew the competitiveness of the New York region in the global economy. Its high degree of connectivity—including high-speed rail links to cities in the megaregion—and its public realm will catalyze the redevelopment of its sad surroundings.

The new Penn Station includes three key pieces. First, a southward expansion of the sweeping but undersized track and platform plan, increasing capacity by 50% to meet the growing demands for service on Amtrak, NJ Transit, LIRR (even with the addition of East Side Access to Grand Central), and Metro-North. Second, the replacement of the miserable basements with a grand civic gateway, full of light and providing the quality of services New Yorkers should expect. Third, the provision of a public realm: sidewalks for people, neighborhood cafes and shops, and places of social interaction that are the 'agora' of the information-age city.

Do we need new tunnels from New Jersey to relieve the bottleneck and vulnerability of our 100+ year-old tunnels? Yes. Do we need to move Madison Square Garden to a nearby site where it too can set a new standard for the 21st century? Yes. Do we need to begin now? Yes.

Why hasn't this happened? We have many conflicting plans and lots of independent authorities. What we need is one shared vision, one implementing authority, and one creative plan for funding and finance. We need to take advantage of this moment to move the Garden and create a new gateway that will move our city faster and forward.

BUILDING A REGIONAL IDENTITY

Next New York:
Air + Rail
March 29, 2013

Participants:
David Bragdon
Joel Ettinger
Alex Garvin
Paul Goldberger
Arthur Imperatore
Deborah Marton
Robert Paley
Sam Schwartz
Marilyn Taylor
Robert Yaro

JOEL ETTINGER: It costs a fortune just to keep what we have in a state of good repair. The interesting issue to me is financing. How do we pay for great projects in the New York metropolitan area?

MARILYN TAYLOR: We are not Denver. We cannot just take twenty-three municipalities, vote on a sales tax, and dedicate it primarily to a single project. We have competing priorities here. We have to think about every single revenue stream that we have and how it is fairly and reasonably divided. We cannot just say, "Oh well, I need $10 billion for the Gateway Tunnel." We have to make the case for it. Only with a shared commitment can we make it happen.

. . .

ROBERT YARO: Until 1989, there were two great world cities with divided transportation systems: New York and Berlin. Berlin fixed their problems but we still haven't fixed ours.

We have three not-quite-competing, but totally separate commuter rail systems that should not be functioning that way. We have underinvested in these systems for decades. And we have a set of institutional challenges. The Port Authority and the MTA were

established to get day-to-day politics out of the business so that we would have freestanding institutions with independent revenue streams. The problem is that both institutions have become intensely politicized. If we were going to build an entity to build the Gateway Tunnel and a new Penn Station, it might look a lot like the Port Authority! It would have to be a bi-state authority.

The key thing here is elevating everybody's sights. We want to maintain the place that New York has in the global firmament, but the reality is that the rest of the world is making these investments and we are not.

London is doing the state of good repair work that we are doing, but they are adding dramatically to the capacity of the transportation systems at the same time. Virtually every other global city is. We have to get out of the paralysis that we are in now. We have to return to the connection between infrastructure and development. It used to be hardwired!

Grand Central and the subway system were real estate scams! These were designed to create value and to capitalize that value into supporting both capital and operating costs. We need

29

to get back to that and to other mechanisms to finance these improvements. I think that this is not a question of if we would like to do one or the other, because we would like to do all of these things. These are all going to be essential to the long-term wellbeing of this city and region.

MARILYN TAYLOR: I truly honestly worry that the 500,000 people who plod through Penn Station everyday have given up hope that it's ever going to be any different. They're just going to hunker down and walk down the corridor as fast as they can with no belief that anything else can happen. We must shift our thinking to what can be possible.

ROBERT PALEY: The question that this raises for me is how do you first build a sense of regional identity? All these issues are fundamentally rooted in the notion that this is one economic region. Institutionally and politically it's not a region; it's a set of balkanized areas. We need to help the public understand that their well-being is connected to the region, not just where they live or work.

. . .

DEBORAH MARTON: I do not think it is just politics that are in the way. There is a kind of regional ignorance about the connectivity of these systems. There has to be greater public knowledge about how these systems work. Unless there is a broad understanding and a clarity of vision, I do not really see us moving forward.

. . .

ALEX GARVIN: We have to face the fact that no regional decisions are going to happen without picking up all of the individual political entities that are involved. The reason that the governors will not do this is that they are not supported in doing this. How do we get to the point where it becomes interesting for the governor of New Jersey to get involved?

ARTHUR IMPERATORE: As far as the ARC tunnel was concerned, Governor Christie was objecting to what a lot of New Jerseyans were objecting to. As heavily taxed people in a very congested state, New Jerseyans felt that they were subsidizing the New York real estate community, and that the overages on the project were going to be borne by New Jersey taxpayers.

SAM SCHWARTZ: I am looking for a new acronym. I have been calling it WIIFM – "What's in it for me?" As I have been going around pitching this idea, people have been saying, "What's in it for me?" A lot of people don't draw relationships to the greater good. We have to show people what's in it for them and for all of us, even if they live in Staten Island or Nassau County.

. . .

PAUL GOLDBERGER: There are two big problems we have touched on so far in this discussion. One is the enormous sense of localism: the failure to see beyond local boundaries to look at these problems regionally. That's not new. But beyond localism, I'm concerned about a much more profound problem that goes far beyond our region, and is relatively new to our age, which is the disinclination to believe in investment—or what we might better call the refusal, or inability, to see infrastructure as a form of investment.

Every day we live on investments that the past generations made for our benefit, building infrastructure even when the economy was in more difficult straits than it is now. They did it then because they felt they had to, and we benefit from that belief. And yet we are doing nothing to follow that same principle today—we are not investing in the future the way the past invested in us. If people were asked every day what they were doing for the next

generation and they were forced to answer "Nothing," maybe the way we view this issue might begin to change.

What ties together all the plans presented here today is that every one of them is doing wonderfully creative things with existing infrastructure. That further underscores the benefit we get from our existing infrastructure. And it makes our disinclination to look forward and see infrastructure as a necessary investment in the future even more disturbing.

I think this really is one of the major American political and cultural problems right now, because it is all about refusal to acknowledge the burden we are placing on future generations if we bequeath to them a nation that is physically crumbling. And even though New York is more inclined to invest in infrastructure than much of the rest of the country is, I think we still have by far the lowest amount of infrastructure investment among the world's most competitive cities.

31

EXPRESS CONNECTIONS TO THE REGION'S AIRPORTS

Grimshaw Architects: Andrew Whalley + Gregory Haley

All three airports serving New York—John F. Kennedy, LaGuardia, and Newark Liberty—are in need of retrofits and greater accessibility. Why not tie the redevelopment of our airports to the development of the greater city?

We need to rethink access to our region's airports within a broader vision for the city's development. The goal of 'Hub City' is to create express connections between the airports and the city's major transportation hubs—Grand Central Terminal, Penn Station, and the World Trade Center Transportation Hub. If we leverage existing infrastructure to create high-speed connections of 30 minutes or less, we can link all three airports and entice travelers to spend some time in Manhattan.

Also, in lieu of an airline ticket, we propose a smart card that operates seamlessly as a ticket to your flight and as a public transportation pass. This would allow travelers a couple of hours in the city to shop, eat and sightsee before jumping back on their flights.

In London, the city utilized existing infrastructure to create the Heathrow Express, which connects you from the airport to the city core in fifteen minutes. Funding was tied to the development of the fifth terminal at Heathrow, lightening the burden on the London Underground and taxpayers.

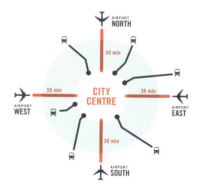

Andrew Whalley is the Deputy Chairman of Grimshaw Architects and represents the Chairman's Office for all international projects. Gregory Haley is a Senior Architect at Grimshaw Architects' New York City office.

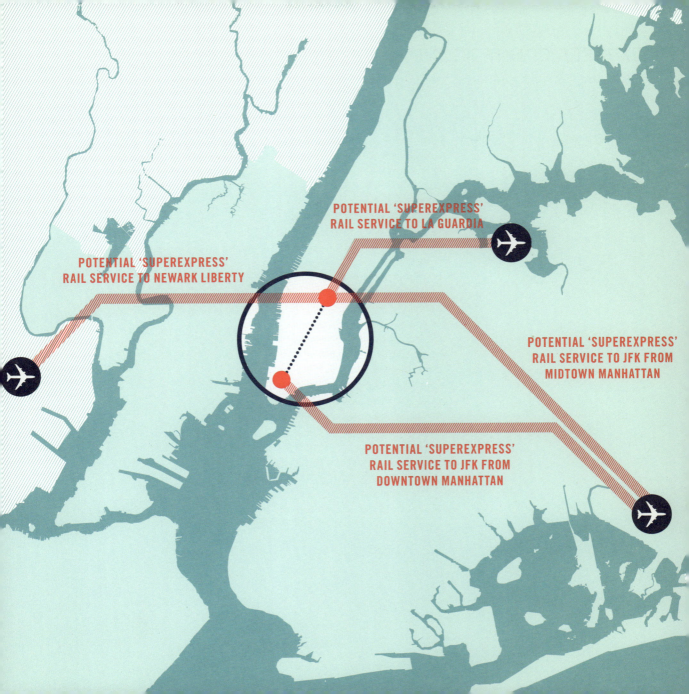

ONE-SEAT RIDE TO LAGUARDIA AIRPORT
Alexander Garvin

Connecting LaGuardia Airport to Penn Station and Grand Central Terminal would require the acquisition of just one lot.

A new rail connection could run express from the tunnels at Penn Station or Grand Central Terminal, via the new East Side Access Tunnels, through Sunnyside Yards toward the Hell Gate Bridge along the same right-of-way. The rail line would pass through one private lot before running along the Grand Central Parkway, then onto Port Authority of New York and New Jersey property, before stopping at each of the main LaGuardia Airport terminals.

The total cost of the rail line would be $1.4 billion dollars, according to a 2005 Parsons Brinckerhoff study.

Alexander Garvin is President and CEO of AGA Public Realm Strategists, a planning and design firm specializing in the public realm. He is Adjunct Professor of Urban Planning and Management at Yale University. He currently serves as the President of the Forum for Urban Design.

SUPERCHARGED TRANSIT CORRIDORS
Claire Weisz, Mark Yoes + Jacob Dugopolski

The New York City streetscape should be designed for increased and evolving modes of transit. Think of it as Complete Streets 2.0: car-free streets with linear parks, protected bike lanes, and mass transit. These kind of parkway connections would contribute to reducing the heat island effect as well as reducing fossil fuel use.

We propose to pair a surface mass transit line—Select Bus Service or future Light Rail—with long-range bike corridors. These streets would be limited to shared vehicles, including taxis, carpools, and electric vehicles. By providing a diversity of opportunities for bicycles, transit, and carpools, we can allow a greater capacity of travellers, new social gathering spaces, and shared capital investment.

Imagine a park on Park Avenue, extending from Chambers Street in Lower Manhattan north to the Grand Concourse in the Bronx. We could link the growing edge of creative workplaces from Sunset Park to Astoria by creating a corridor along 3rd Avenue, Park Avenue, Marcy Avenue, and 21st Street. We could complete a major corridor along Brooklyn's Atlantic Avenue to provide a direct link to the waterfront from Barclays Center. And finally, we could create a continuous greenway link along the East River in Manhattan, from Battery Park to Sherman Creek.

Claire Weisz, FAIA, and Mark Yoes are Founding Principals of WXY Architecture + Urban Design, a New York-based firm focused on social and environmental transformation of the public realm at multiple scales. Jacob Dugopolski is an Architectural Designer and Project Manager with WXY.

BUILD A BUS RAPID TRANSIT NETWORK
Ben Fried

Ben Fried is the Editor-in-Chief of Streetsblog, a national blog network for sustainable transport, smart growth and livable streets.

NYC Department of Transportation's "complete street" redesign of First Avenue—a dedicated bus lane, a pedestrian refuge, and a protected bike lane—carries more people in the same space as a regular avenue. Since they installed it in 2010, biking is up almost 50%, bus speeds are up 18%, bus ridership is up 10%, and traffic injuries are down. New York needs overhauls like this on many more streets in every borough. Queens Boulevard, for example, is the classic example of a street that's dangerous and inefficient because it's only designed to move cars.

I propose that we re-design our wide, car-centric streets as true transit boulevards. This is a concept that goes beyond the Select Bus Service (SBS) model that the City and MTA have used so far. Painting bus lanes and collecting fares before passengers board have sped up SBS routes, but New York can do better. We need to build a world-class Bus Rapid Transit (BRT) network. Boarding platforms should be located in the center median of major two-way boulevards, sheltered from the elements, and level with bus doors for faster boarding. Bus passengers should get to bypass traffic congestion without getting blocked by double-parked cars or turning motorists.

Other American cities are leapfrogging us. Chicago is moving forward with a true BRT corridor on Ashland Avenue. It will not only serve as a more efficient means of transportation, it will be an economic development tool for neighborhoods underserved by transit. Let's not fall behind Chicago. Neighborhoods in every borough will have better access to jobs and opportunities if we transform their wide, dangerous streets into pedestrian-friendly transitways.

Part of the appeal of Bus Rapid Transit is that it can respond to the growth in travel demand, which is increasingly intra-borough and inter-borough, not involving Manhattan... BRT would supplement corridors that are vastly underserved in terms of high capacity transit, such as Jamaica to Flushing, where most of the growth is going to occur.
  – David Bragdon

BIKE SUPERHIGHWAYS
Paul Steely White

With the successful launch of North America's largest public bike share system, Citi Bike, it is increasingly apparent that New Yorkers are embracing bicycling as an everyday mode of travel, especially for trips of two miles or less. But, for longer commutes, New Yorkers still lack adequate infrastructure. With the exception of the Hudson River Greenway and a few other continuous bicycling rights-of-way, long bicycling trips are hampered by frequent stopping, unsafe intersections, and circuitous routing.

Bike superhighways, or 'bike rapid transit,' present a welcome solution to speed long-haul bike journeys in New York City. Already emerging in other world-class cities, bike superhighways are wide, continuous protected bike lanes with prioritized, unbroken rights-of-way. In Copenhagen, bike superhighways are supported by stoplights that are timed by bicycling speeds of 12-13 mph. With this kind of infrastructure, bicyclists could travel on longer, faster, and safer bike trips into the central business district and between boroughs.

One potential candidate for bike rapid transit is Queens Boulevard. The wide median along the boulevard's 7.2 mile length is ideal for housing a wide, two-way bike superhighway. With bike-friendly signal timing, this corridor could speed thousands of commuters a day between Manhattan and the easternmost reaches of the city.

While the Bloomberg administration has taken huge strides in improving our city's streets, the Department of Transportation has only begun to consider bike rapid transit as an option. We will need the help of the next mayor to make this a priority for our city's infrastructure.

Paul Steely White is the Executive Director of Transportation Alternatives, the leading local advocacy group for bicycle, pedestrian, and transportation reform in the United States.

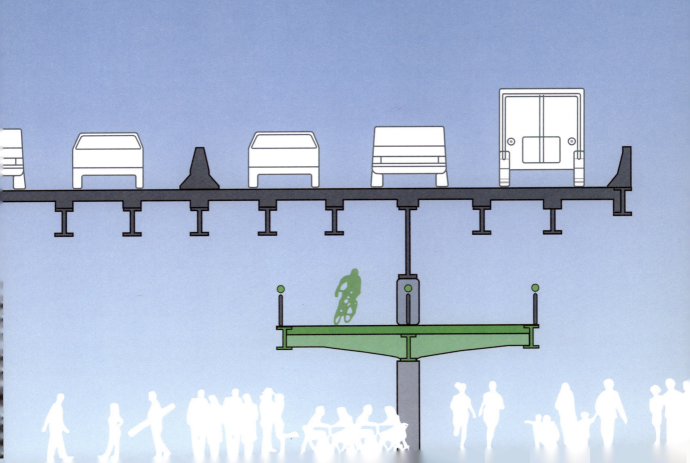

STREETS FOR THE TWENTY-FIRST CENTURY

Next New York:
Roads + Bridges
May 3, 2013

Participants:
David Bragdon
Adam Forman
Roxanne Warren
Claire Weisz
Robert Yaro

DAVID BRAGDON: Part of the appeal of Bus Rapid Transit (BRT) is that it can respond to the growth in travel demand, which is increasingly intra-borough and inter-borough, not involving Manhattan. In other words, much of the growth in travel demand is not associated with the same armatures of the radial subway system. This BRT would supplement corridors that are vastly underserved in terms of high capacity transit, such as Jamaica to Flushing, where most of the growth is going to occur. That's a really important demand in advocating for this network.

We should also keep away from a debate about the choice of vehicle, pitting BRT versus Light Rail versus streetcar. We should really focus on the advantages to the user regardless of which of those three modes is used, which is partly a right of way design issue. Features like the station area design, the off-vehicle payment, and most of all, the separated right of way, translate to speed and reliability for the user whether it is BRT or Light Rail.

ROXANNE WARREN: I agree that we should consider banning cars from certain streets. With our high percentage of transit usage in this city and the fact that, in Manhattan, only twenty-three percent of households even own a car, we should be combining auto-free streets with transit.

ADAM FORMAN: What about Green Streets? We should think of more ways that green space can protect bike lanes while capturing rainwater and relieving the sewer system. This will demand significant coordination between the Department of Transportation, the Department of Parks and Recreation, the Department of Environmental Protection, the Municipal Transportation Authority, Con Edison, and Verizon. I am wondering how to coordinate these city agencies and state agencies in order to build truly complete streets.

ROBERT YARO: That could be one of the priorities for the next mayor.

One of the things we heard today is a really outlandish idea that Park Avenue ought to have a park in it.

CLAIRE WEISZ: A "supercharged" Park Avenue could connect all the way to the Grand Concourse, which is another example of how new transit routes could be inter-borough.

ROBERT YARO: Many of our boulevards and wider avenues could, in fact, become park avenues and multi-modal routes.

44

I like thinking about how we can incorporate the next generation of infrastructure and get these streets built in a coordinated way. It just drives me crazy in this town when you see the number of times utilities will rip up the streets and then the city will come and do the same thing!

. . .

We really need to be planning for a polycentric city which is not all about getting in and out of Manhattan. Getting out of Manhattan is another thing we need to be thinking about, but we should be thinking about inter-borough routes as part of a broader economic development strategy for the city.

CLAIRE WEISZ: We have a real issue to grapple with in bringing roads and bridges design to the larger consciousness. This is such an important issue, and it is probably one of the most exciting topics for the future of public space. Not enough people understand that streets compose the largest percentage of New York City available to the public. It is sort of like the human skin, which never gets any recognition as the largest organ of the body.

ROBERT YARO: It's not an accident that the radio stations do traffic and weather together. These are the two systems that we assume there is nothing you can do, other than knowing what might be coming your way. You assume that there is going to be weather and that there is going to be congestion. That could change!

DAVID BRAGDON: So are you saying that every ten minutes they should do a traffic and land use report?

ROBERT YARO: There is a whole new world of opportunities that we can bring to the next mayor.

ACTIVATE THE QUEENSWAY
Laurie Beckelman

The next mayor should redevelop the abandoned LIRR Rockaway Beach Branch into a cultural greenway for Eastern Queens. Partially elevated and partially subsurface, the greenway would extend 3.5 miles from Rego Park to Ozone Park and would serve 140,000 residents within a ten-minute walking radius and an additional 250,000 people within a mile.

Drawing on the success of the High Line, this greenway could transform an eyesore into a rich resource for the community. The programming opportunities are incredible: walking, jogging, cycling, public art installations, multi-ethnic food festivals, concerts, teaching gardens, lectures and yoga, among many others.

Supporters have created "Friends of the QueensWay" and enlisted the Trust for Public Land to study its feasibility. The challenge is raising the money to build it. It is in Queens, not Manhattan, and it does not share the same sexiness or appeal of development as the High Line. And yet, it fits well within the goals of PlaNYC 2030 by creating a green space and cultural resource for the outer boroughs. The next administration should do everything in its power to transform this idle infrastructure into a thriving amenity.

Laurie Beckelman is a Founding Partner of Beckelman+Capalino, which provides a wide range of project management and strategic advisory services to cultural, not-for-profit and historic preservation clients.

EXISTING

PROPOSED

CAP THE BROOKLYN-QUEENS EXPRESSWAY
Susannah Drake

In Williamsburg, there is a tremendous opportunity to cap the trench of the Brooklyn-Queens Expressway and build an open space amenity for the South Side Williamsburg community. This is not a tunnel and not a "Big Dig." Instead, it is a thin deck capping the BQE that could benefit over 160,000 people in the surrounding neighborhood, which is a primarily low-income and Hispanic area.

Aside from the benefits to the community, there are a number of economic benefits in capping the trench with a park. Increases in the land value, retail value and property taxes in the surrounding area could cover as much as 75% of the cost of the park alone. There is potential for new construction jobs and other related economic activity during construction.

Furthermore, the bridges crossing the BQE were built 50 years ago and are reaching the end of their lifespans. The City will have to spend $30 million on their replacement in the next five to ten years. We should leverage that local expenditure against a federal ask for an additional $70 million in funding. If we can secure that funding through a HUD community development grant or other infrastructure initiative, we can transform this piece of crumbling infrastructure into an incredible new open space for the community.

Even in Dallas, they've covered over the freeway that runs into Downtown Dallas to join a business district with a residential district. And that was a very elaborate "covering over." This is much less expensive. I think that this could be a signature project for the next mayor.
— Adrian Benepe

Susannah C. Drake, FASLA, is the Founding Principal of dlandstudio, an award-winning multidisciplinary design firm. She is also Visiting Professor at The Cooper Union.

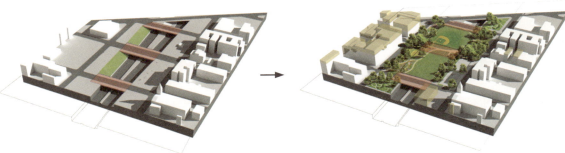

LEVERAGE NECESSARY BRIDGE RENOVATIONS AND
INCREASED REAL ESTATE VALUE INTO NEW OPEN SPACE

LET THE WATER IN
Chris Reed

Water needs more space in the city. Over the past centuries, rivers, floodplains, and protective wetlands have been continually filled in or moved to make room for urban growth. This work was done with a mindset that once the water is taken away, it would not come back. We know better now.

In giving back space to water, I don't mean to fully displace urban and social uses. In fact, reintroducing natural systems can bring new life and richness into the public realm. Fish parks, bobbing buildings, water plazas, canal streets: all can be designed to recognize both civic and hydrologic functions, and nod to their watery origins.

We can also transform vacant land into new wetlands—whether within the city (for stormwater and runoff) or at the edge (for tidal flux, sea level rise, and storm surge). Stormwater detention basins, small-scale rain gardens, and seawalls can now be re-thought and expanded into large-scale ecological parks that bring value to adjacent neighborhoods.

Perhaps we can go further, integrating water into the fabric of the city itself. Public plazas, waterways, and boulevards in new or re-tooled neighborhoods can be designed to be floodable green infrastructures, creating new open space connections that could also work as elevated escape routes in the event of an emergency.

Importantly, these strategies require a shift in thinking—we need to adopt an amphibious mindset. And they point to new coordinated, integrated, interdisciplinary, and collaborative roles that our public agencies can play in remaking the city.

Chris Reed is Founding Principal of Stoss Landscape Urbanism and Associate Professor in Practice of Landscape Architecture at the Harvard University Graduate School of Design.

RIPARIAN BUFFERS ALONG THE BROOKLYN WATERFRONT
Maria Aiolova and Mitchell Joachim

How can we protect the Brooklyn waterfront from the threat of future storms and rising sea levels? We propose that the City investigate the adaptive reuse of former military vessels to create a riparian buffer zone that confronts the issues of storm surge and flood management in the New York Harbor.

Our concept is to recycle ghost fleets or vessels from the National Defense Reserve Fleet (NDRF) and United States Navy. The vessels could be cut apart, cleaned, and used as riparian buffer zones to absorb large charges or surges in flooding areas. We could then combine natural sedimentation with the recycled ship parts to restore the natural water edge and slow down the watercourse. This aqueous zone would allow for a programmatic mix—recreational opportunities paired with natural stormwater retention.

As we reimagine the waterfront, we need to design infrastructure that lets the water in, rather than keeps it out. New York does not need to defend against water but instead share its presence with the existing estuary.

Maria Aiolova and Mitchell Joachim are Co-Presidents of Terreform ONE (Open Network Technology), a non-profit design group that promotes green design in cities. Aiolova presently chairs the ONE Lab NY School for Design and Science. Mitchell is also Associate Professor at New York University.

FLOATING ISLANDS
Mark Thomann

We propose to create a green edge of floating islands around Manhattan. A network of artificial islands is a productive, attractive, and cost-effective approach to create ecological infrastructure and new public space. Just as the great Aztecs produced agriculture on floating chinampas, or Bangladesh created societies around floating gardens, or just as Thailand's floating markets attract tourists and drive the local economy, floating islands could be the future of open space in New York City.

There are several ecological benefits to a network of floating islands. The island module is expandable and flexible—it can be deployed to protect the city from storm surge and accommodate the rising sea level. They can be designed as a network of landscaped sponges that filter and clean the river. They can even provide a framework for new infrastructure to capture tidal energy.

Moreover, we can begin to look at their potential as productive agricultural spaces. The City could even develop a new market for specialty produce. There is a delicacy, La Bonnotte potato, from Île de Noirmoutier, an island situated off the Atlantic Coast of France, that grows specifically in salt water.

Finally, and most importantly, they can provide fun and exciting opportunities for recreational public space. We imagine a network of islands equivalent to the size of Central Park around Manhattan. Like Central Park, this landscape will serve as a productive landscape infrastructure and innovative public space model for coastal cities in the 21st century.

Mark Thomann is the landscape design director with Balmori Associates where he has led the conceptual design and development of numerous international projects and strategic plans. He is on the Landscape Architecture faculty at the University of Pennsylvania School of Design.

ATTRACTING DIVERSITY IN AN AFFLUENT CITY

Next New York:
Arts + Culture
May 17, 2013

Participants:
Deborah Berke
Susan Chin
Adam Forman
Hugh Hardy
James Sanders
Carol Willis

SUSAN CHIN: What we are lacking is a discussion about how New Yorkers are advocating for more arts and culture as we see a shift from finance to more diverse industries.

We need to continue to attract people who are making things, who are creative. How do we create enough affordable space for those people to continue to be a part of that industry? How do you provide housing for young creators to bring new energy to the city?

. . .

CAROL WILLIS: We should recognize that the arts are entrepreneurial in nature. The arts may be populist, but they are not likely to be voted upon by a majority. So, should the function of government be to facilitate the entrepreneurial nature of the arts, rather than to ensure funding and investment in areas that need to be contested by different groups?

HUGH HARDY: That is something for the next administration to wrestle with, and it is our job to try and inform them.

. . .

ADAM FORMAN: I want to introduce a little nostalgia for the bad old days. What the 1970s offered was art movements with proper nouns. Not just culture, but cultural movements, whether it was Punk Music, or Pop Art, or Hip Hop.

I think a key element was the fluidity between boroughs and between income levels. The Bowery was a focal point and laboratory to propagate Hip Hop music from the South Bronx, or graffiti from Brooklyn. There was real integration of culture and of class that in many ways has been lost.

Some consider Williamsburg and Bushwick the city's newest cultural pivot. But I strain to think of a proper noun that has come out of Brooklyn, except for 'Brooklyn' itself. What's missing is geographic, racial, and economic diversity. I am wondering what arts planning can do to improve integration among boroughs, incomes, and ethnicities.

Toronto is very good about public arts investment because they index it to local income levels, and they are very intentional about dispersing it among a variety of neighborhoods.

JAMES SANDERS: I think you are right. But I think that the 1970s had 'privileges' that we no longer enjoy. The city had contracted and that had left huge areas which were formerly very active economically and

57

58

industrially—including the Bowery, the South Bronx, and Brooklyn. The rents were low and hardly anybody lived there or even wanted to live there.

That provided an opportunity for all sorts of things. Whether it was Hip Hop coming out of the housing projects in the South Bronx—where no one would ever live if they did not have to—or the Bowery, which was a very self-selected community: a very small group operating in the East Village, because nobody else wanted to live there and the rents were low. We do not have that privilege anymore.

We now have the opposite problem, which is a city that is outwardly incredibly successful and naturally everybody is talking about unaffordability. That is the price of success! If people did not want to live here, the prices would be lower. The price of success of New York in the last 15 years is now a challenge that we have to confront.

For 25 years, New York was hunkered down and not thinking about the future. The city was contracting. What new buildings were you going to need for a contracting population?

DEBORAH BERKE: I want to build on something that James said: We've got it good, compared to the secondary and tertiary cities in this country, who would do anything to have New York's problems. We have tourism. We have culture. We have extraordinary philanthropy. We have lots of rich people. We have visibility. Our problems get focused on and we attempt to get them solved. Other cities have the problems of New York City in the 70s, and they'd love to be like us.

We need to think even bigger and reach out beyond the boundaries of New York City. 'No Longer Empty' should share exhibitions done here with cities that don't have arts capital. Maybe library courses could become online courses for cities that can't fill their libraries with programs. Maybe the 7 Line should be extended to Pittsburgh and beyond! Let's think and plan and act regionally, even nationally.

If we think only about our backyard, we are losing urban capital that is building nationally. And in working with other cities, we can help them, and they can help us, and we can be about cities, not just our city.

EMBRACE MODULAR CONSTRUCTION
MaryAnne Gilmartin

Since the 1870 introduction of the elevator transformed New York from a city of walk-ups to a city of high-rises, we have seen remarkably little change in the construction industry, even as we have developed better materials, more sophisticated technology, and a smarter means of enhancing building safety.

Modular construction can transform how we build affordable and market-rate buildings with greater savings and a diminished impact on the community and the environment. At our first high-rise project at Atlantic Yards, we found that we can use a modern means of construction while embracing sustainability and delivering on world-class architecture.

Modular units can be built in an off-site facility with all final finishes installed, like flooring, fixtures, appliances, and facades. And because modules are built indoors without risk of height hazards or inclement weather, we can forge new partnerships with union labor to build more safely and cost-effectively. Once on site, modules can be bolted or press-fit together and facades are designed to lock into one another without any on-site work. And because modular buildings are assembled faster, the community is less impacted by construction noise and traffic.

This new means of construction could be a critical component of a greater strategy to address affordable housing in this city. At our Atlantic Yards project, we estimate that modular construction will generate 20%+ savings on a compressed timeline. We estimate 70-90% less waste and 67% lower energy consumption. By using modular construction to build quickly, densely, affordably, and sustainably, we can radically shift how we build great cities.

The one limitation in bringing it to the site is the width of the road and the height of underpasses. You must stay within those limitations... You can't build a theater in one piece. Housing in New York, however, can be built that way.
  – Theodore Liebman

MaryAnne Gilmartin is President and Chief Executive Officer of Forest City Ratner Companies, a New York-based real estate development company. She has been point person in the development of several high-profile real estate projects in New York City, including Barclays Center at Atlantic Yards, The New York Times Building, and New York by Gehry.

MODULES ARE CONSTRUCTED USING UNION LABOR IN A UNION FACILITY

BROOKLYN NAVY YARD FABRICATION FACILITY

SAFER CONDITIONS ON THE FACTORY FLOOR THAN ON-SITE

ACCURATE QUANTITY-TAKE OFFS AND PRECISION CUTS FOR REDUCED WASTE

MODULAR UNITS LEAVE THE FACILITY AS FULLY FINISHED APARTMENTS WITH FIXTURES, APPLIANCES, CABINETRY AND ATTACHED FACADE

2.4 Miles

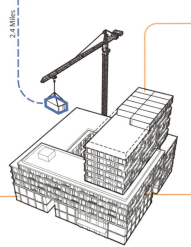
PROJECT SITE

SHORTER CONSTRUCTION DURATION AND FEWER DELIVERIES REDUCE NEIGHBORHOOD IMPACT

SELF-HEALING FACADE PANELS INTERLOCK WITH ADJACENT MODULES, ELIMINATING ADDITIONAL ON-SITE WORK.

ALL MODULE CONNECTIONS ARE BOLTED OR PRESS FIT FOR STREAMLINED ASSEMBLY

RE-SKIN PUBLIC HOUSING
Fred Harris

Fred Harris is the Executive Vice President of Development of the New York City Housing Authority (NYCHA). He previously served as the Senior Vice President of Development for AvalonBay Communities. The views expressed herein are those of Mr. Harris, not NYCHA.

Most of NYCHA's buildings are 50-75 years old with billions of dollars in deferred maintenance. There's a capital investment backlog of $6 billion today, increasing at a rate of $3 million daily. Rent from NYCHA residents covers at most 50% of the operating budget. So while NYCHA is a great success—providing housing for 1 out of 13 New Yorkers—it is also struggling to remain solvent. The habitability of its buildings will soon be threatened if capital investments are not forthcoming.

I propose to locally manufacture and apply new skins to the facades of our aging public housing stock. These skins would contain space to replace plumbing and electrical infrastructure and add new through-the-wall PTAC heating and air conditioning units and insulation without having to disturb residents' apartments nor to remove or extensively repair the existing brick facades. I estimate that the cost of re-skinning would amount to about $100,000 per apartment, or $17.8 billion for all NYCHA properties. (Additional money would be needed to renew apartment interiors and replace central plants.)

This program could essentially finance itself through savings from electricity alone. NYCHA residents without electric meters use 6,750 kWh a year on average, whereas the average rental in the Northeast uses 4,513 kWh a year. By halving the electric utility bill, we could save about $200 million a year, which could support as much as $5 billion of investment. If it were possible to resell electricity which NYCHA secured years ago for what is now a very low price, a similar amount could be generated. Proportionally, even greater savings would come from heating through the potential decline in NYCHA's annual gas and oil expenditures.

AFFORDABLE HOUSING FOR YOUNG NEW YORKERS
Robert C. Quinlan

New York must entice talented newcomers by offering them truly affordable housing. I propose to rezone outer borough manufacturing areas that adjoin emerging residential neighborhoods as micro-housing enclaves.

Micro-Apartments, measuring between 250 and 370 square feet, have become an accepted idea. The City is exploring amending Department of Building regulations to accommodate micro-housing citywide. Yet the prototype in Kips Bay championed by the Department of Housing Preservation and Development estimates monthly rents ranging from $940 to $1,800. We must create new housing with monthly rents no higher than $1,200 to attract innovative New York newcomers with technical and artistic skills to the city.

Under this proposal, the city would rezone manufacturing areas in the outer boroughs like Bushwick, Gowanus, Red Hook, and Long Island City to allow for micro-housing development. These are outlying areas where studios, sound stages, and nightlife are already emerging, largely without existing housing. This rezoning should not mandate costly residential amenities like community rooms and in-house gyms. Younger residents of small living units will seek to spend more time outside, animating the surrounding streets with cafes, beer gardens, and delis.

In addition, the City must create an incentive for developers and lenders by reviving the successful J-51 Tax Exemption Program. Eliminating property taxes for ten years will dramatically lower annual carrying costs, enabling developers to pass the reductions through to tenants in their rent. A ten-year tax exemption would motivate banks to lend in these emerging areas without affecting a developer's cash flow expectations.

Robert C. Quinlan is Principal of Quinlan Development Group, a New York City-based real estate investment and development firm that he founded in 1971.

INVIGORATE OUR PUBLIC LIBRARIES
David Giles

As New York City continues to adapt to the needs of an information-based economy, the demand for life-long learning resources has never been greater. At all ages and educational levels, New Yorkers are looking to upgrade their skills in order to make use of new technologies and market themselves more effectively to employers. Public libraries are the city's most important resource for non-institutional learning, whether it be English language workshops for immigrants, after school programs for kids, or computer classes for seniors.

With 206 branches across the five boroughs, New York City has a tremendous physical legacy to build on, but the vast majority of branches are in desperate need of upgrades. Many Carnegie buildings were designed for solitary readers rather than classes and group work. Dozens of old branches have underutilized floors, many with shuttered custodial apartments, that could be tapped for new uses, including small business incubators, co-working spaces, community rooms and classrooms.

In partnership with New York's three library systems—New York (Manhattan, the Bronx, and Staten Island), Brooklyn, and Queens—the city should increase the general capital allocation for libraries and issue a $500 million bond to fund capital projects across the city. The libraries could aim to raise another $250 million through private donations and philanthropy to underwrite the city's first comprehensive capital plan for libraries since Andrew Carnegie's initial bequest over 100 years ago.

With community input, a citywide plan could help all three systems realize efficiencies through branch consolidations, storefront expansions (so-called flex spaces with lower overhead) and mixed-use developments that incorporate affordable housing.

David Giles is the Research Director at the Center for an Urban Future, where he has written extensively on a variety of public policy issues including transportation, technology and the arts.

IMPROVEMENTS TO CITY OPERATIONS

Could city government be better equipped to confront the challenges of a growing population, ailing infrastructure and rising tide? How might city government streamline regulatory processes to stimulate growth? And how can city government better capture the value of public assets to maintain and enhance the public realm?

The following ideas are a collection of proposals for improvements to city operations. The views expressed are those of the contributors and do not reflect the opinions of the Forum for Urban Design.

THE NYC DEPARTMENT OF FOOD
Thomas Jost

In the same way that New York City dedicates itself to building its water and waste infrastructure, we must recognize the importance of food to our health, security, and economy.

I propose the creation of the New York City Department of Food to oversee food security, improve public health, grow the regional food economy, and put New York on the path toward a more sustainable future. There is a significant market for locally supplied food in New York City. And, while there are ample farms and capacity for significant growth, upstate farming communities lack the processing and distribution infrastructure to effectively "ramp up" the supply into New York City.

Currently, about 14% of the city's food is sourced locally. New York City can create a graduating locally sourced food contract through major city institutions such as public prisons, schools and hospitals. This would enable farmers to "plan" for growth based upon a recognized demand and increase investor willingness to construct the necessary infrastructure to support that growth.

Another challenge is efficient distribution. The State of New York should work to support the development of privately-operated collection, processing and distribution centers located proximate to concentrations of farms and ranches. A similar distribution network should be replicated within New York City, with a contracted operator providing storage, resorting, packaging and local distribution to end users through a fleet of energy-efficient vehicles organized to optimize final delivery. Through distribution infrastructure and an organized marketing effort to connect farmers with consumers, NYC can link the city marketplace with upstate food producers who do not yet have the business infrastructure to connect effectively with urban consumers.

This system of creating a market, building the necessary infrastructure, and connecting farmers with consumers will restore a sustainable farming economy in New York State with New York City benefitting from a lowered carbon footprint, reduction of truck traffic on City streets, greater access to local food, and a healthier diet.

Thomas Jost is a Senior Urban Strategist at Parsons Brinckerhoff, a global consulting firm assisting public and private clients to plan, develop, design, construct, operate and maintain thousands of critical infrastructure projects around the world.

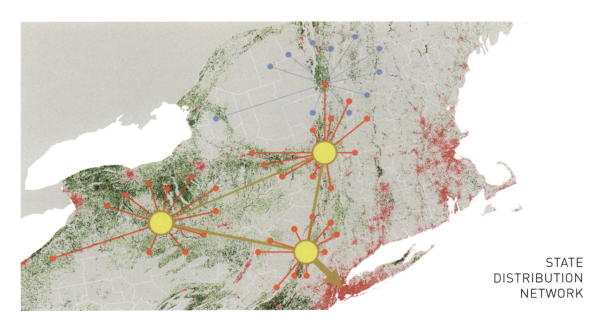

STATE DISTRIBUTION NETWORK

CITY DISTRIBUTION NETWORK

RESTORE THE CAPITAL BUDGET TO CITY PLANNING
Ronald Shiffman

The next mayor will need to move quickly, decisively, and transparently to face the pivotal issues left unaddressed over the last two decades. Whether it is to sustain Mayor Bloomberg's signature achievement — PlaNYC2030—and his coastal recovery and adaptation strategy; to address his failure to accommodate the city's homeless population; or to confront the 'sorting' of the city that is pushing the poor to the periphery, the next administration must aggressively engage New Yorkers in a coordinated and participatory way. The ability to plan, prioritize, and apply capital infrastructure expenditures—subject to the participation of the public and consent by City Council—will be essential.

NYC residents and businesses need to help set the framework for public and private investment; otherwise, land use decisions are liable to languish in courts for years. The framework for participatory planning exists in the City Planning Commission and our ULURP process. However, the capital budget powers of the Planning Commission were removed at the time that ULURP was strengthened, which has relegated City Planning to being a responsive agency unable to effectively engage in the planning, adoption, and implementation of mayoral-, agency-, or community-initiated plans.

We must restore the capital budget powers to the City Planning Commission. It is one of the few City entities with a charter mandate to engage the public. If that engagement is linked to reinvigorated citywide and community-based planning processes, maintained by a properly staffed agency that works directly with strengthened community boards, the City Planning Commission can become the proactive, independent and sustained force we need to address critical climate change and equitable development challenges facing the city.

Ronald Shiffman is a city planner with 50 years of experience providing planning and development assistance to community-based groups in low- and moderate-income neighborhoods and a former member of the City Planning Commission (1990-96). He is a Professor at the Pratt Programs for Sustainable Planning and Development and the Founder of the Pratt Center for Community Development.

REFORM THE LANDMARKS PRESERVATION COMMISSION
Steven Spinola

Steven Spinola is President of the Real Estate Board of New York, the real estate industry's leading trade association in New York City.

The landmarks system is broken. First, there is a serious lack of transparency surrounding landmark and historic district designations. The Landmarks Preservation Commission has the ability to designate substantial portions of the city as historic districts without justifying their rationale before they act. It can also shelve decisions for decades, creating de facto designations. And it is not required to issue design guidelines for historic districts that describe which windows, storefronts, entryways and cornices are permitted in these distinct sections of the city, unfairly burdening and confusing property owners.

Second, let's stop pretending landmark designations are always used to protect our city's cultural heritage. The curtain has come down on why so many historic districts have been designated in recent years. Preservation advocates have stated clearly that landmarking is a planning tool that can be used to stop or redirect development. We have to think about how to preserve the City of New York's future, not just its buildings.

We therefore propose that the Landmarks Preservation Commission be placed under the management of the Department of City Planning. City Planning has the ability to examine every aspect of development citywide, including the city's housing, economic development and open space. The Landmarks Commission, on the other hand, cannot consider any of these aspects that are essential to the success of the city.

We should not landmark away the economic vitality of New York City. Let's reform the Landmarks Preservation Commission and empower the Department of City Planning to make those decisions.

FOUR FORMULAS FOR SENSIBLE DENSITY
Mark Ginsberg

There's a tremendous need for more density in the city. Our population is growing, and we're projected to reach 9 million in 2030. When the Zoning Resolution was passed in 1961, it estimated a full build-out of 12 million. With underbuilt sites across the city, the final build-out will likely be closer to 10 million. We don't have more land, so we need greater density.

First we need to implement a 20% optional FAR bonus for inclusionary housing in R6 and above residence districts. Although this is now being done on a case-by-case basis, this could be a citywide strategy to significantly up-zone while encouraging the production of affordable housing.

Second, we need to expand the use of unconventional housing. We can explore 250-400 sq. ft. micro-apartments in developments citywide. We can legalize shared units, so that more than three unrelated people can live together legally. And we can legalize accessory units. There are as many as 100,000 illegal units in Queens alone—we can create policy so extended family could live in basements or adjacent units.

Third, the City should begin purchasing and redeveloping low-density housing. There are abundant opportunities where one-family houses could be redeveloped into multi-family walkups. "Towers in the park" projects could also explore infill housing to help fill our critical need.

Finally, when a community votes to downzone a neighborhood, city officials should respond by asking, "Where will you upzone to balance the loss?"

We also need to come up with a program that would mandate some low-income or middle-income housing in buildings throughout the city of New York that no longer work and could be converted to create more housing.
  – Steven Spinola

Mark E. Ginsberg, FAIA, is a founding partner of Curtis + Ginsberg where he has led award-winning residential, institutional, and urban design projects. He is President of Citizens Housing and Planning Council, and past President of the American Institute of Architects New York Chapter.

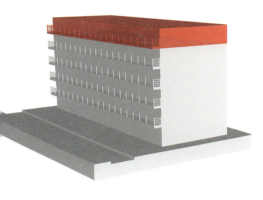

20% FAR BONUS FOR INCLUSIONARY HOUSING IN R6+ DISTRICTS

LEGALIZED SHARED AND ACCESSORY HOUSING

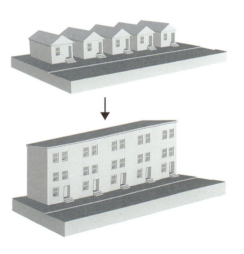

REDEVELOPED LOW DENSITY HOUSING

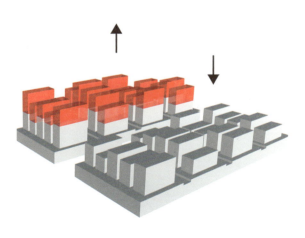

BALANCED ZONING

STREAMLINE AFFORDABLE HOUSING EXEMPTIONS
Kathleen Dunn

Kathleen Dunn is a Principal at Dunn Consulting and Development where her work has focused on affordable housing development and urban planning. Ms. Dunn is also Adjunct Assistant Professor at the NYU Wagner School of Public Policy.

Since the federal government withdrew direct subsidies for affordable housing development about three decades ago, the City of New York has relied on three main vehicles to preserve or develop affordable housing: low-cost land, grants and low-interest loans, and tax abatements and exemptions. The City has successfully streamlined the delivery system for land sales and making grants and loans. But tax abatements and exemptions remain tangled.

The City of New York has claimed, in a number of different venues, that they are exploring permanent affordability programs for housing, yet there is no tax abatement program that provides benefits to owners of that housing in perpetuity. Currently, there exists an array of programs with different terms and recipients. The housing finance program, for-profit or not-for-profit status of the developer, and whether a project is new construction or rehab lead each project down a different path. The process is taxing and does exactly the opposite of what it should do—it drives development costs up.

The City should create one tax abatement and exemption program for affordable housing. If our primary goal is to create more low- and moderate-income housing that lasts, we can do that better with one simplified program. The term of that tax abatement should be equal to the length of the regulatory agreement that it complements. The additional cost to the City should be nil.

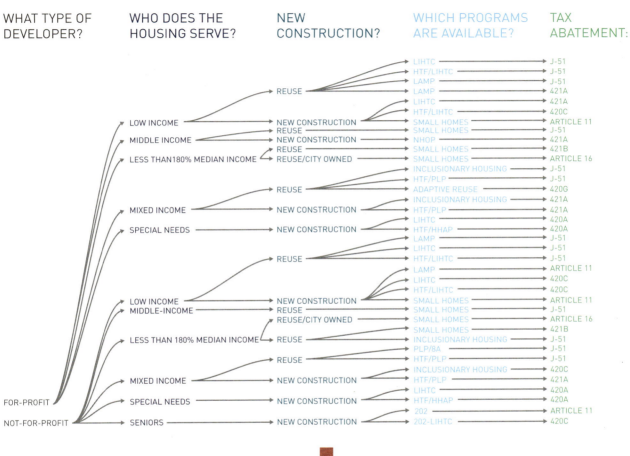

MAKE ROOM FOR MIDDLE-INCOME HOUSING
Steven Spinola

Steven Spinola is President of the Real Estate Board of New York, the real estate industry's leading trade association in New York City.

We have a serious shortfall in housing. Our total population is expected to rise by another million by 2030. The vacancy rate has stayed below 5% since it was first recorded in the 1960s. And half of New Yorkers pay more than 30% of their income on housing. The costs of construction and the regulatory processes are extremely high in New York City, and property owners are paying as much as 30-36% of gross income in taxes. When the tax exemption expires in many of the properties in the 80/20 Housing Program, property owners will likely convert to condos since they can no longer maintain the rentals as low-income housing.

We propose to create a new tax exemption program that addresses the City's affordable middle-income housing needs. We propose implementing a new housing program for families making 80% of the average median income (AMI) or higher. Currently, the 80/20 Housing Program offers affordable housing to families living in the 40-50% AMI range, but we need to broaden our definition of affordability. Higher AMI for some units should be permitted in exchange for a greater percentage of affordable units, as done in Williamsburg.

Furthermore, we need to consider how to extend the 20-year tax benefit schedule. A 25-year tax benefit schedule would provide sufficient benefits to build and operate the affordable units during the exemption period. And with a fair and predictable real estate tax, perhaps capped below 25% of gross revenue, we could extend the middle-income housing benefits in perpetuity.

REWRITE THE REQUEST FOR PROPOSALS
Carol Lamberg

Carol Lamberg is the Executive Director of the Settlement Housing Fund. She has over 40 years of experience as a housing professional, and is an expert at conceptualizing new projects and programs in housing legislation. Lamberg also co-chairs the New York Housing Conference and is Regional Vice President of the National Housing Conference.

The affordable housing industry has mushroomed. Many qualified organizations compete whenever a government agency invites proposals and announces that subsidies or tax benefits are available. Typically, developers spend six months preparing responses to requests for proposals (RFPs). This has never been easy, but in recent years, the requirements have become extremely complex, arduous and expensive. Losing competitions is painful.

Typically, approximately 30 documents are required, including detailed architectural submissions and financial projections. The developer must show combinations of subsidy and tax abatement to achieve affordable rents, and many sources are only sporadically available. Because it is challenging to document all the funds, an alternate "as-of-right" proposal is required. Many unfeasible proposals are submitted. Government agencies take a long time to select a winner. Construction and operating costs rise. Design changes and new financial arrangements are inevitable.

It is time to streamline the process. An applicant would provide the track record of the development team, a zoning analysis, a short narrative, schematic plans and a preliminary financial projection. City agencies would provide a preliminary commitment to the winner and subsequently require advanced drawings, firm cost estimates, disclosure statements and community approvals.
The developer would complete arrangements with banks, other funders, and investors, and would add amenities and programs, if appropriate. The architect would complete construction drawings and obtain a permit. The closing celebrations would come next.

If the RFP process were simplified, we would have more time to advocate for funds and create more affordable housing and better programs.

A NEW GENERATION OF CONSTRUCTION TRADE WORKERS

Donald Capoccia

Donald Capoccia is the Managing Principal and Founder of BFC Partners, a real estate development company focused on the production of affordable housing.

Construction costs are one of the most significant barriers to the production of affordable housing. The NYC Prevailing Wage for electricians, carpenters, plumbers, and laborers is double or triple the wage costs to employ these tradesmen in the greater metropolitan area. Quite simply, that increases the cost of producing affordable housing by up to 30%.

Because this is housing targeted to specific income bands, there is no ability to increase debt when using conventional financing, which is often found in the capital structure of affordable housing projects. As such, in order to finance the additional costs required by prevailing wages, government is required to provide those additional funds. Given the environment of restricted and constrained government resources, the only result of this is a reduction in the number of units that can be produced. If all projects were subject to the NYC prevailing wage, you would likely cut production in half.

As developers of affordable housing, we have been struggling with the cost of producing affordable housing for many years. We have aimed not only to meet a critical demand for housing in NYC, but also to rebuild challenged communities. In order to do so, many developers have devised ad hoc recruitment and training programs to offer job opportunities to unemployed neighborhood residents. We must broadly expand this work under the leadership of our next mayor.

The next mayor must mandate a labor partnership that includes REBNY, NYSAFAH, the Building and Construction Trades Council, CUNY, and NYCHA to address the needs for construction cost containment and the increased demand for affordable workforce housing. Our aim should be to invest in training and supporting unemployed and underemployed New Yorkers from transitioning neighborhoods where the majority of affordable housing is being built, and provide an economically sustainable pathway for a new generation of construction trade workers.

EMPOWER SHARED RESOURCE MODELS
Elliot Felix

Elliot Felix is the director of Brightspot Strategy, where he leads projects that create brighter work and learning experiences by improving space, services, technology, process, and culture.

We have a tremendous opportunity to achieve economic, social, and environmental sustainability by promoting the shift from ownership to membership models. Membership models enable people to share resources they might have previously had to own. And while there is an emerging movement to share resources (in programs like Citibike or General Assembly), the city must do more to allocate new spaces to shared uses and foster the development of membership-based service models.

The city should build on successful precedents so that people can share not only apparel, tools, toys, and bikes, but space as well. Sharing space results in greater potential for interaction among people, reduction in material and energy use, and access to services that might be otherwise unavailable. New York City should incentivize property owners and developers to allocate a greater percentage of spaces to co-working, shared meeting and educational facilities, and incubators.

Shared spaces will only work if they use the right service model to recruit, support, and retain members—be they individual entrepreneurs, growing companies, or large universities. Therefore, New York City should provide expertise in service design, business modeling, and community management—three essential ingredients for successful shared spaces. Finally, New York City should explore opportunities for shared spaces to act as community hubs with access to shared goods and services, such as tool libraries in shared fabrication labs or business modeling in co-working spaces.

By encouraging the shift from ownership to membership, New York City can lead the way in the experience economy, creating opportunities for communities to interact, share resources and ideas, and achieve environmental sustainability.

REDUCING THE COST OF NEW HOUSING

Next New York:
Housing
April 26, 2013

Participants:
Richard Anderson
Daniel Brodsky
Donald Capoccia
MaryAnne Gilmartin
Steven Spinola
Carol Willis

RICHARD ANDERSON: One thing that wasn't mentioned was the cost of government review and approvals. New York is the only place in the country that has an industry profession called expediters, and we know why. Would not this be a fruitful area for a new mayor to get into – how can we streamline, how can we reduce the cost of government review and approvals in the overall development process?

DANIEL BRODSKY: That's one of my favorite subjects. Constantly, when we confront the City about excessive bureaucracy, officials respond by saying that these are safety issues or corruption issues, so therefore we have to have more people and more processes.

I think we all want to build safely and no one wants corruption. But, I think we also all want a more efficient government.

. . .

CAROL WILLIS: I wonder if we could bring together the idea of density that Mark Ginsberg suggested with some other integrating of mixed-uses. When you densify neighborhoods by rezoning areas that need new housing and commercials uses, there could be a targeted community development

approach that would cross agencies. Not just Housing (HPD) or the Department of Buildings (DOB), but as a City Planning initiative.

DONALD CAPOCCIA: We have spent many billions across the city in a number of emerging and challenged neighborhoods. Some of those neighborhoods have done very well, and others haven't performed to expectations.

We have to take a close look at those neighborhoods that didn't do as well and understand what is missing. When a public investment has been made in those neighborhoods, we now need to consider funding mixed-income and mixed-use projects aggressively, including providing for daycare centers and neighborhood retail. These are all components of a healthy neighborhood, which will ultimately attract market activity to these neighborhoods, as we have so clearly seen in Harlem, Downtown Brooklyn, and other locations that previously seemed unappealing.

STEVEN SPINOLA: I want to make two more suggestions. First, we have many buildings that are overbuilt in the city. There ought to be an automatic grandfathering of buildings to be able to knock down, modernize, and build anew.

81

82

Second, there is no program right now for the conversion of obsolete office and industrial buildings to make them into housing, which is probably the most inexpensive way of doing it.

We need to come up with a program that would mandate some low-income or middle-income housing for buildings throughout the city of New York that do not work anymore; they could be converted to create more housing.

MARYANNE GILMARTIN: The City's housing programs presently incentivize based on unit count, not the size of the units themselves. Therefore, there is no incentive built into the system to create larger family units for middle- and low-income housing. We are looking at micro-units for market-rate housing, and I think that gets to the way that people want to live, work, and play in a mixed-use, dense environment.

For affordable workforce housing and family housing, the housing needs to be suitable for families. We need to address the fact that there is no incentive to build larger family units on affordable housing. You are simply penalized in the layering in of incentives. If there is a wholesale look at the way incentives work in the next administration, which is an

absolute need, then that will help to develop the kind of affordable housing that this city needs.

THE CZAR OF PUBLIC SPACE
Lance Jay Brown

Walking along 23rd Street from Chelsea to the Flatiron district I come across an ever more complicated agglomeration of open spaces and attendant furnishings. There are sidewalks, subway entrances, and streets that serve all traffic from trucks to cyclists to pedestrians of all stripes. There are news boxes, parking meters, hydrants, streetlights, waste receptacles, bus stops, and trees. There is the charming hodge-podge of pedestrian plazas at the 5th Avenue-Broadway intersection filled with periwinkle umbrellas, planters, and moveable chairs. To the east is Madison Square Park, a beautiful open space animated by public art, Shake Shack, lawns, dog runs, and a children's playground.

The pedestrian plazas and Madison Square Park are divided not only by fencing, but also by the authorities that maintain them. The Department of Transportation rules to the west and east of the park and the Parks Department rules in between. The MTA, Con Edison, water, sewer, cable and other utilities rule below. Such is the case citywide.

Who is in charge of all this? How is it that adjoining public spaces are controlled by different agencies? Why is everything so "zoned"? Why can't utility excavations and modifications be completed simultaneously rather than sequentially?

Our overriding priority must be the public arena, the actual public space itself, the space we all own. And one department or commission should be responsible for its design, coordination and development. We need a Commissioner of the Public Realm, a Coordinator of the City Surface, a Director of Public Space!

Lance Jay Brown, FAIA, is a New York-based architect, urban designer, educator, and author. He is the principal of the award-winning studio Lance Jay Brown, Architecture + Urban Design, founded in 1972 and is the AIANY President-Elect 2014.

FOSTER HEALTHY, INTEGRATED COMMUNITIES
Ronald Shiffman

Ronald Shiffman is a city planner with 50 years of experience providing planning and development assistance to community-based groups in low- and moderate-income neighborhoods and a former member of the City Planning Commission (1990-96). He is a Professor at the Pratt Programs for Sustainable Planning and Development and the Founder of the Pratt Center for Community Development.

The planning policies that we have undertaken over the past three decades have led to greater income segregation citywide. At the same time, there is growing recognition in the health field that segregated cities are unhealthy, not just for the poor who bear the brunt of living in often substandard conditions, but for the wealthy and all other income groups as well. We must recognize that the process of displacement and replacement now occurring citywide will not foster integrated and healthy communities, and we must explore new zoning mechanisms to reverse this pattern.

First, we must pursue policies and interventions that protect against displacement. We should explore the implementation of mandatory inclusionary housing in all new developments through new tax abatements and other forms of public subsidies for building owners and developers. Moreover, we must develop a series of procedures to vigorously enforce fair housing statutes.

Second, we must provide housing for all income groups in proportion to their need. Currently, our affordability standards are based on the Standard Metropolitan Statistical Area median income, which measures regional income and raises the boroughs' averages dramatically. I propose to base our affordability standards on borough median income figures so that no community is developed to benefit any group over another on the basis of income, race, or class—though exceptions may be made where there is an affirmative obligation to overcome previous exclusionary practices.

If the city continues to move in its recent pattern where Manhattan becomes an island for the super rich, we will have developed a sophisticated form of economic apartheid and will suffer the consequences of a less healthy city.

DYNAMIC ZONING
Jonathan Rose Companies: Will Goodman

The static nature of the zoning code can make it an ineffective tool in helping communities address changing needs and conditions in their neighborhoods. It's time to create a more dynamic planning process that explicitly addresses community well-being, not just form.

The next mayor should endeavor to create a nimble and responsive system that continuously collects data on performance and feeds it back into the planning process. As communities set goals for the well-being of their human and natural systems, emerging "Big Data" tools now enable us to get real-time feedback about the outcomes of development decisions and continuously adapt policy accordingly.

For example, neighborhoods could establish parking standards based on quality-of-life goals like walkability, bikeability, street vitality, and commercial presence. Communities could then collect real-time parking and mobility data and revisit zoning parking requirements each year based on current patterns. The city could tie this to a dynamic pricing system that increases prices during peak times to meet mobility goals.

Community health is another example. If a neighborhood is struggling with child asthma rates, it can set a reduction goal and use planning tools to address it. The zoning code could limit certain uses that create health hazards, and owners could gain "use it or lose it" density bonuses by retrofitting buildings using non-toxic materials, natural ventilation and green roofs.

Zoning is important, but it cannot achieve comprehensive results without being used in concert with other planning and policy strategies, including building codes, incentives, and investments in infrastructure. The key is creating a dynamic system that is always adapting to community needs and that features increased collaboration among a range of agencies (City Planning, Housing, Transportation, Energy, Health, Education, etc.) to achieve common goals.

Will Goodman is the Chief of Staff for Jonathan Rose Companies, a leading green real estate development, investment and project management firm based in New York City.

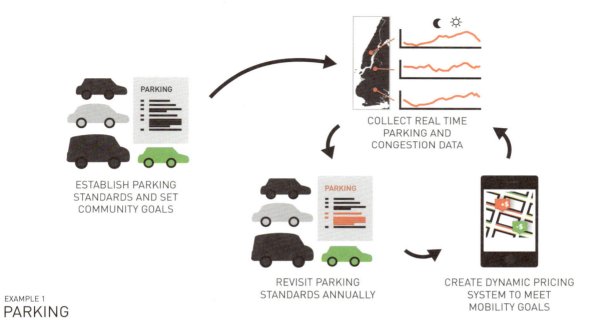

EXAMPLE 1
PARKING

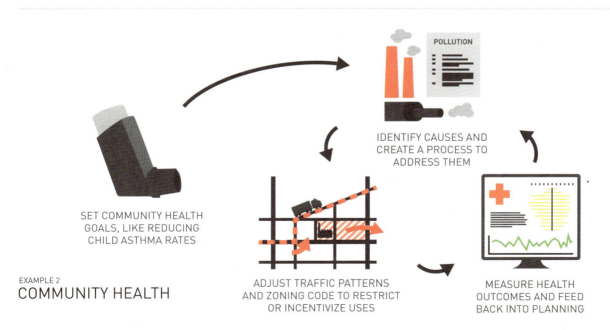

EXAMPLE 2
COMMUNITY HEALTH

87

VERTICAL URBAN FACTORIES
Nina Rappaport

How can we encourage manufacturing to take root in our city and thrive? Historically, factories provided stable jobs and built the urban economy. With the advent of containerization and the digital supply chain, factories left for cheaper land and labor in free trade zones with few human rights. Furthermore, New York pushed out manufacturing by shrinking or eliminating its industrial zones.

Where can a manufacturer go if they want to build here? Is the city flexible enough to provide spaces to manufacturers hoping to reshore? City government must recognize industry's potential to create high-paying jobs with skilled labor and the pride of "working in place."

The City should aim to create vertical urban factories. I propose the City convert M1-1 zones into multi-storied M1-4 zones to increase the value of manufacturing sites and spur taller development in both new and existing buildings. Second, sustainable industrial designs concepts could be promoted along with EDC's existing loan programs for manufacturers to improve their spaces. Third, industrial uses should be integrated into mixed-use neighborhoods. New smaller-scale, clean, green, and robotic manufacturing enables us to live with side-by-side spaces for making. Finally, manufacturing needs to be made visible. This might be a physical change, like encouraging larger windows in the Garment District, or a marketing approach, like expanding the Made in NYC program.

The factory, once inspiring in its architectural innovation, must be considered equally significant today. Reinventing the factory has the potential to engage the public in the cycles of making, consuming, and recycling needed to create a self-sufficient city.

NYC is successful because there is still some manufacturing here. The Garment District, the industry maybe least appropriate for Midtown, still exists because of protective zoning. Now we are seeing cutting-edge fabrication and design there. We don't have to allow NYC to become completely deindustrialized.
 – Tobias Armborst

Nina Rappaport is an architectural critic, educator and curator of the traveling exhibition and forthcoming book, *Vertical Urban Factory*. Rappaport serves as Publications Director at the Yale School of Architecture and editor of the biannual publication *Constructs*.

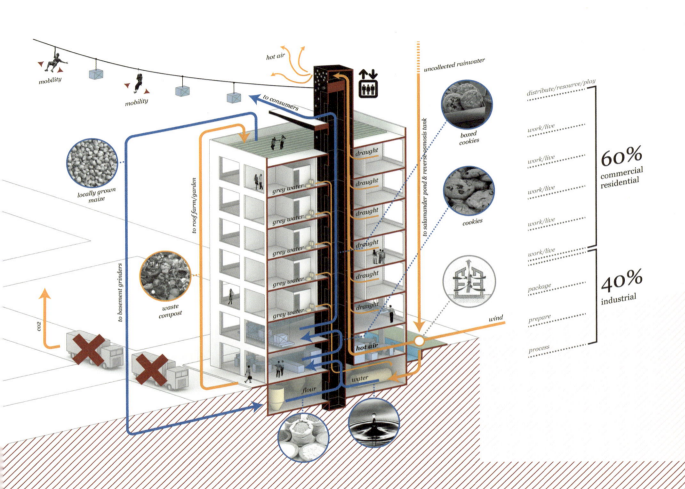

LEVEL THE TOLLS
Sam Schwartz

Robert Moses built the bridges and tunnels where we pay tolls today within the five boroughs. Nelson Rockefeller, as governor, created the MTA in 1965 and took the excess revenue to pay for transit shortfalls. There's no other rhyme or reason for it. If we started all over again, we wouldn't put tolls on the Throgs Neck, Verrazano or Rockaway bridges to pay for a radial subway system that goes to the Central Business District. Let's be fairer about it.

I propose lowering the tolls at all the outer crossings—Throgs Neck, Whitestone, Triborough Bridge, Verrazano and Rockaway bridges. Let's return the East River bridge tolls (removed by Mayor William Gaynor in 1911) to the level that they are at the Battery Tunnel or the Queens Midtown Tunnel to prevent "bridge shopping". And let's introduce a charge at the 60th Street grid line by EZ Pass or license plates. No tollbooths need be constructed.

When commuters contribute to the congestion they create, the end result will be about $1.5 billion per year in new revenue. I would recommend directing a third of the revenue toward maintaining a state of good repair in the transit system, and two-thirds toward capital improvements of our transit and highway systems.

The will to implement this could come from the outer areas, where we lower the tolls and from the downtown areas of Brooklyn, Queens and Manhattan where traffic will be relieved and transit improved. By bonding this at $12-15 billion dollars to start, we could create 35,000 recurring local jobs!

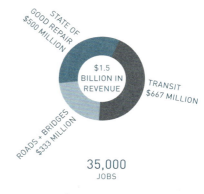

Sam Schwartz is President and CEO of Sam Schwartz Engineering (SSE), a firm that specializes in transportation planning and engineering. He also writes a column on traffic for *The New York Daily News*, has a column in *Transportation Technology International*, and blogs for *Engineering News Record*.

EXPAND LANDMARKS' ABILITY TO TRANSFER AIR RIGHTS
Vicki Been

The historic preservation regulations governing New York City's landmarked buildings make it costly for owners to maintain their buildings and can render buildings impossible to renovate or sell. Acknowledging the unique burdens placed on landmark owners, the city instituted a development rights transfer program in 1968 that allows landmark owners to transfer unused development rights more widely than other property owners. However, because the required review process is lengthy and uncertain, few transfers have occurred since the program's creation.

Given the tremendous contribution that landmarks make to New York City, we need a more effective program to allow property owners to use untapped development rights to obtain funds needed for maintenance. We propose amending the zoning text to allow non-profit landmarks to transfer their development rights anywhere within their community district, as of right, as long as the development rights can be used within existing building height and setback constraints. Increasing the market for development rights would create value for cash-strapped landmarks, enabling them to maintain their buildings without sacrificing their mission. The program could also impose a fee on transfers for use by the local community or create a fund to help maintain landmarks throughout the city.

Everyone in the city benefits from the preservation of landmarks, but only owners bear the cost of preserving them. Let's create a process that—by appropriately increasing density—enables landmarks to sell unused rights to raise the necessary funds to maintain their historic buildings.

The transfer fee could be used to improve the capacity of local infrastructure or to improve the streetscape by adding parks — appeasing and actually enriching the community.
  – Adam Forman

Vicki Been is the Director of the Furman Center for Real Estate and Urban Policy. Additionally, she is the Boxer Family Professor of Law at New York University School of Law and an Associate Professor of Public Policy at NYU's Robert F. Wagner Graduate School of Public Service.

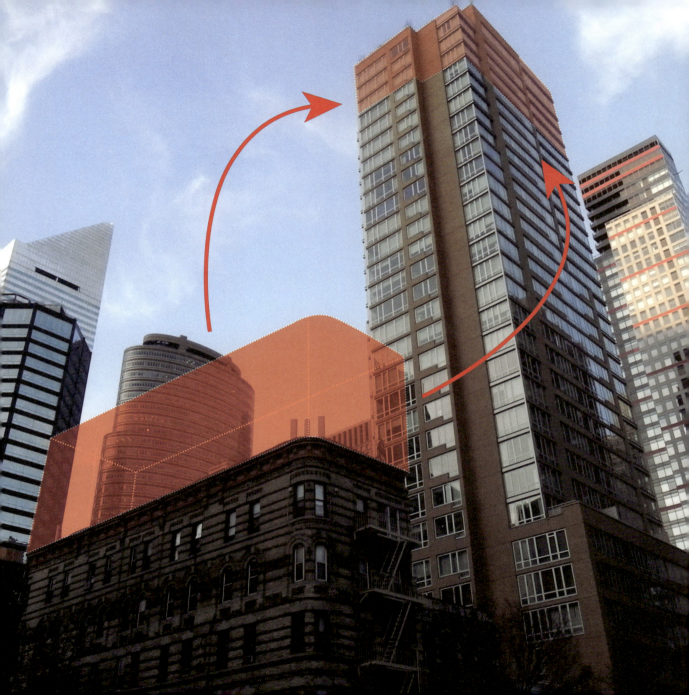

USING ZONING TO FOSTER VIBRANT COMMUNITIES

Next New York:
Zoning + Development
April 5, 2013

Participants:
Daniel Brodsky
Mark Ginsberg
Meredith Kane
Will Goodman
Theodore Liebman
Andrew Lynn
Ronald Shiffman
Marilyn Taylor

MARILYN TAYLOR: Should we start thinking about shifting what zoning does? Should we get rid of the concentration on the tiny details, which we may not actually need anymore? You know, the 800+ pages of the New York City Zoning Resolution contains a lot that we don't need if we really shift to a focus on results rather than regulations.

RONALD SHIFFMAN: What we attempted in the community's proposed 197a plan for Williamsburg was exactly that. We proposed taking the King-Spadina zoning model up in Toronto and applying it in New York. The idea is simple: you set performance standards, you create the envelope, and you let the developer do whatever it needs within that as long as it's predictable. You could increase densities here or there, but you could also do a lot of other things as long as you achieve both the urban design goals and the community goals.

WILL GOODMAN: I don't even know if the 800 pages of environmental impact statements ask the right questions. It's so unwieldy it becomes almost impossible to change. We should start to really just think about performance and outcomes and start by asking: what are the outcomes that communities really want? What is a healthy community? What are the social, environmental and economic components that we really want to start shooting for?

THEODORE LIEBMAN: New zoning should benefit from hindsight. We have made big mistakes in quantifying everything for the sake of ease, rather than set out to create qualitative performance standards that truly improve how we live in our cities.

MARK GINSBERG: Zoning is a tool of planning. Shouldn't we be first talking about comprehensive planning? Maybe one could argue that PlaNYC is the closest thing that the city has to a comprehensive plan. We need to be talking about citywide issues and zoning individual communities as one component.

DANIEL BRODSKY: I agree with you; zoning is just one tool. We should first consider the outcomes and then establish what the zoning should be.

RONALD SHIFFMAN: Zoning really should allow you to build to the carrying capacity of the social, economic and physical environment. If you then allow a bonus above that, you are overburdening the existing infrastructure. Two examples are parts of the Williamsburg

95

96

waterfront and the proposed Atlantic Yards development. The only other possibility is to reduce the maximum and then to reach the maximum when you transfer development rights, which is unfair to the development community. We should begin to think about what the maximums should be given the infrastructure—transportation routes or street capacity, for example.

Sometimes, by the way, we build too low as was the case in Community Board 4 in the Bronx and parts of East New York and the Broadway Triangle in Brooklyn.

. . .

MEREDITH KANE: What the City has done, and it's been an interesting approach, has been zoning that builds up with incentives, where you're not just rewarding the property owner with windfall on an upzoning, but you're actually using zoning as a tool to create value for the public. Basically, the City is having developers buy increased FAR, whether through a transfer fee or by building required improvements, and so is therefore using upzoning to create the public realm that we want.

. . .

ANDREW LYNN: You ought to plan the transit before you upzone, but it's often hard to know what to expect.

RONALD SHIFFMAN: I always like to think of the sign along the train lines to East New York. It said: Lots for Sale. The train helped develop East New York. If you look at what developed the Grand Concourse, it was the train line!

ANDREW LYNN: One example where that recently worked very well was the 7 Train extension.

RONALD SHIFFMAN: Given Sandy, and given the fact we need communities in this region along the coast to work together, why isn't the Port Authority being talked about as a robust vehicle for doing much of the planning for the region? I remember when the Port Authority funded some of the planning studies in Long Island City to look at how the waterfront should be developed.

The Port Authority has a key role here to play because they're the one entity that bridges New Jersey and New York, and they really can begin to bring the two states together and deal with some of the issues that we're going to have to deal with over the next decades when we're addressing climate change!

97

LEVERAGE OUR VACANT SPACES
Naomi Hersson-Ringskog

Vacant buildings and storefronts are detrimental to the health and vibrancy of our city. Too often landlords do not take advantage of the incredible opportunity that their vacant spaces could provide to artists, entrepreneurs and small organizations. We need to begin harnessing the potential of underutilized space citywide.

"Creative interim use," or filling empty spaces with arts and cultural programming, is an adaptive and powerful strategy. It's timely—you can occupy a vacant space for two weeks or six months. It's scalable—you can inhabit storefront windows or create immersive exhibitions. It's resourceful—we're using existing buildings and sometimes making them better for future uses. And it's flexible—vacant spaces can be transformed with food, technology, and other productive public uses.

The City should create a comprehensive and publicly accessible database that tracks public and private vacancies. The mayor should appoint a manager to cut through red tape and facilitate access to empty spaces. And finally, the City should create a tax incentive to encourage the transformation of these spaces. This could take the form of a tax abatement for property owners who volunteer their spaces, or a tax penalty to get property owners to the table.

The difficulty is that every property owner likes to think that their space will be rented tomorrow. Nobody wants to give it over for that 3 or 6 months, which you really need to make this a success. However, if your city policy could give a real estate tax break when vacant spaces are donated to the arts, there would be greater incentive.
  – Meredith Kane

Naomi Hersson-Ringskog is Executive Director of No Longer Empty, a not-for-profit organization that seeks to widen public engagement with contemporary art, to promote the work of experimental and socially-conscious artists, and to build resilience in communities.

5,000 GREENSTREETS
Nette Compton

There are countless paved areas of our roadbed that are sitting idle, devoid of beauty and serving little purpose. Through the Greenstreets program, and most recently in partnership with the Department of Environmental Protection (DEP), we have been converting these eyesores into green infrastructure that absorbs stormwater while providing a pleasant experience for pedestrians, a safe driving route, and new habitats for plants and wildlife. By thoughtfully designing these spaces to mimic natural systems, Greenstreets require minimal care and have a low burden on our maintenance infrastructure.

Green infrastructure is most effective as a network of functional green spaces woven into the fabric of the urban environment. This decentralized approach translates to the improvement of the everyday life of New Yorkers citywide, in the spirit of MillionTrees and Schoolyards to Playgrounds.

New York has plans for sewer overflow abatement via green infrastructure for approximately half of the city, but we need to consider how to implement these programs citywide. A 5,000 Greenstreet program across the remainder of the city where these installations are feasible would have a considerable impact: increasing green space by 160 acres, lessening the impact of the urban heat island effect, absorbing increasingly intense storms, and improving the everyday life of New Yorkers.

Last year during Superstorm Sandy, one greenstreet absorbed every drop of the storm—over 40,000 gallons of water in one 1,500-square-foot site. This type of infrastructure is essential to alleviate the impact of extreme events like Sandy as well as incremental climate changes projected in the coming decades.

Nette Compton is Director of Green Infrastructure at the New York City Department of Parks & Recreation, a division devoted to designing engineered landscapes that transform unused areas of New York into vibrant urban ecosystems. Image: New York City Department of Parks & Recreation.

TRANSFER DEVELOPMENT RIGHTS TO UPLAND AREAS
Susannah Drake

I propose that the city transfer development rights from Zone 1 Flood Zones to upland areas in order to finance a buyout of the city's most vulnerable coastal areas. Governor Cuomo has proposed a buyout of some of these coastal zones, but there is no long-term mechanism to pay for it. This strategy could be used especially to transfer density from residential and industrial zones with low maximum FAR to upland sites.

A share of the value captured by this transfer of development rights should be dedicated to creating a fund for construction and long-term maintenance of wetland buffers and maintaining coastal landscapes. The expense associated with these waterfront buffers slows, delays, and often kills these green infrastructure projects. By pairing development funds with coastal green infrastructure strategies, the city would be able to more easily finance a more resilient and better protected coastline.

Susannah C. Drake, FASLA, is the Founding Principal of dlandstudio, an award-winning multidisciplinary design firm. She is also Visiting Professor at The Cooper Union.

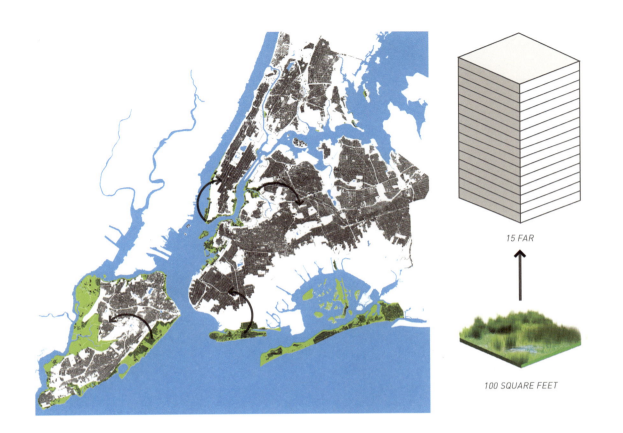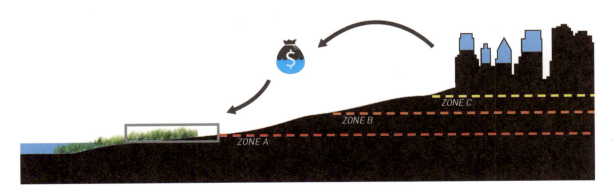

SOCIAL IMPACT INVESTMENT IN PARKS + OPEN SPACES
Deborah Marton

Municipal budget structures and political cycles favor new construction and inadequately fund park maintenance. The difference can be extreme—the capital budget for the Parks Department is $1.3 billion and the maintenance budget is about $300 million. And though a state of good repair may be less sexy than a ribbon-cutting, thriving open spaces provide long-term social benefits like community resilience and improved public health.

Park maintenance must be understood as an issue of equity. Capital dollars can be accessed with relative equality for new work, but the same cannot be said for maintenance dollars, which increasingly come from neighbors and philanthropies. While conservancies may work well in neighborhoods abutting Central Park and along the High Line, they don't work in lower-income communities like Inwood or Corona, where parks suffer from neglect.

I propose the City create 'social impact bonds' to leverage private sector capital to finance critical improvements in our city parks.

Clean and safe open spaces can create great savings for city government by lowering rates of obesity, lowering crime rates, or protecting low-lying communities from flooding. If we can monetize the benefits of open space for public health, as well as offset disaster relief expenditures with the savings generated by resilient green infrastructures, we can begin to fund maintenance today.

If we are a truly racially, ethnically, and economically diverse city, we have to make sure a shared vision of our city exists not just for our wealthiest citizens but for our low-income communities as well.

If you look at the overall economic impact of well-maintained open spaces and how they can help forego healthcare costs, then you could also consider the negative impacts of a bad park. A poorly maintained park brings down the value of the neighborhood. It is like the public space-equivalent of having foreclosed homes sitting on the block.
    – Connie Fishman

Deborah Marton is the Senior Vice President of Programs for New York Restoration Project, a nonprofit organization dedicated to reclaiming and restoring New York City parks, community gardens and open space.

SOCIAL IMPACT BONDS

PARK MAINTENANCE FUNDING

LOWER HEALTH CARE COSTS AND INCREASED TAX REVENUE

SAFER, HEALTHIER PARKS

HAPPIER, HEALTHIER COMMUNITIES

CAPTURE THE VALUE OF OUR PARKS + PUBLIC SPACES
Madelyn Wils

Madelyn Wils is President and Chief Executive Officer of the Hudson River Park Trust, a State authority responsible for developing, managing and operating the 5-mile long, 550-acre waterfront park.

Even though the City has created dozens of waterfront parks in recent years, there has been no thoughtful, comprehensive, and long-term vision for park upkeep citywide.

When the City plans to create a new open space or waterfront park, they negotiate with the Parks Department and real estate developers to secure maintenance money. Those agreements rarely yield enough to cover critical investments, like pile or bulkhead repairs. And though parks have an enormous impact on the surrounding community, they rarely capture the increased real estate value.

One solution for existing parks that cannot meet their maintenance needs is the "Neighborhood Improvement District," which we have proposed for Hudson River Park. Borrowing from the Business Improvement District model, the proposed district would assess a nominal fee—15 cents per square foot for commercial real estate, and 7.5 cents for residential real estate—from property owners within a two-block radius of the park.

When developing new parks and open spaces citywide, the City should explore the use of tax-increment financing (TIFs). TIFs set aside future increases in property taxes to subsidize development. The increase in property value is substantial—at Hudson River Park, the value of adjacent properties jumped over 100% from 2003-2007, 20% of which can be directly attributed to park development.

We need to find a way to build out the waterfront, not retreat from it.

THE VALUE OF THE PUBLIC REALM

Next New York:
Parks + Open Spaces
May 10, 2013

Participants:
Connie Fishman
Alex Garvin
Meredith Kane
Andrew Lynn
Deborah Marton
Michael Sorkin
Madelyn Wils

DEBORAH MARTON: We have to monetize the value of parks. The New York Presbyterian Hospital has recognized that the services that they deliver and prescriptions you get from the hospital are not adequate if you are not seeing the impact, particularly in low-income communities. So they are moving beyond the boundaries of the hospital to partner with affordable housing developments, for example, to improve air quality within homes, because they know health is not just what gets delivered in the hospital.

I would suggest that the next step in that progression is to move beyond the hospital. Where health care really gets delivered is the landscape. Those services can be thought of as savings for the future that can fund work right now.

. . .

MICHAEL SORKIN: Air rights are the urban equivalent of printing money and the Planning Department functions as the Federal Reserve, manipulating supply. I wonder if there's a way in which we can monetize – and support – our parks by using them to establish a kind of environmental gold standard. If air rights were fully fungible and based on the fixed amount of open space the city controls, a market would be created that would both fund the

parks and set limits on growth that were derived from an idea about a rational ratio of public and private space and a balance between building and environment. I'd be interested in seeing a calculation of the FAR derived from calculating the total area of building in the city in relationship to the total area of parks.

MADELYN WILS: Hudson River Park is very unusual because technically it is zoned mostly M2-3, so it actually has zoning rights, which were restricted in the 1998 legislation. We are actually working out how to get those Air Rights back for the purpose of selling them. Why are we doing that? Not so much for the maintenance dollars, although that would be helpful. We need a minimum of $275 million to finish the park. At the rate that we are getting money from the State and the City, that is not happening in my lifetime. We are going to have to figure out how to get the capital funds we need to build out the park.

Unfortunately, most of the land across from the park has already been built, but there are still some sites that are not, so air rights are a very big part of our issue. Parkland has no air rights, so there is no transferring from parkland to adjacent property. The Department of City Planning could offer a special permit or upzoning, which could provide millions of dollars in air rights. It seems the value of that should go into improving our public spaces.

MEREDITH KANE: A lot of the recent re-zonings have done that for capital money. For example, there was a transfer of air rights to Williamsburg Waterfront as developers funded waterfront improvements. The High Line zoning has done that – developers pay into a fund that is reserved for construction of the High Line. Hudson Yards is also using that strategy to fund the open space. It funds the capital but not the operating expenses, which is the general difficulty that everyone is facing here. There are so many public goods that are competing for that operating money.

ANDREW LYNN: While there are a lot of public goods, how do you decide which ones benefit from the creation of air rights and set aside real estate taxes? There are two that make particular sense: one is mass transit and the other is parks. With respect to zoning, there are actual improvements in that area that enable you to have a denser neighborhood.

. . .

CONNIE FISHMAN: If you look at the overall economic impact of well-maintained open spaces and how they can help forego healthcare costs, then you also need to consider the negative impacts of a bad park. A poorly maintained park brings down the value of the neighborhood. It is like the public space equivalent of having foreclosed homes sitting on the block.

ALEX GARVIN: The problem you raise is acute because derelict parks are frequently in areas where low-income people live. The problem is that not only do they not have the money to contribute to a surcharge, but also, you cannot charge the owners of the property around it. That is why we have a Parks Department that covers the whole city.

If you offload Central Park, Bryant Park, Battery Park, and a whole series of parks that can support themselves with Tax Increment Financing (TIF) or community districts, you have to be willing to put up money in the Central Parks Department out of the regular budget, because those communities will otherwise never get the service. It is too easy to say that we are simply going to monetize the development rights near something that is very valuable, whether it is the Hudson River Park or Central Park.

DEBORAH MARTON: Our Parks Department cannot maintain all the parks across the city, particularly parks in the lower-income communities. The social cost of derelict parks is a cost we all bear. The health impacts of our poorest citizens are costs we all bear together. We should figure out a way to understand those future costs as current savings and use that to invest in the care of neighborhoods where there are not private dollars.

IMAGE CREDITS

PAGES

16, 17 (Images) Forum for Urban Design
18 (Map) Forum for Urban Design
19 (Image) WXY Architecture + Urban Design
21 (Map) Forum for Urban Design
22 (Map) Forum for Urban Design
23 (Images) courtesy of Alex Garvin
25 (Map) Forum for Urban Design
(Images) left to right: Doug Kerr, Section 215,
Rachel So, George Rex, Guillermo Varela,
Ed Mustapha, Shinya Suzuki, Randy Lemoine,
Dysanovic, Andrew Steinmetz
27 (Images) courtesy of Marilyn Jordan Taylor
32, 33 (Images) Grimshaw Architects
35 (Map) Forum for Urban Design
36 (Map) Forum for Urban Design
37 (Images) WXY Architecture + Urban Design
39 (Image) Kohn Pedersen Fox Associates
41 (Image) courtesy of BrightNYC team from the New
Amsterdam Bike Slam (Michael Mandiberg,
Shachi Pandey, Wendy Schipper, Carmen Trudell,
Stefan Verduin, and Claire Weisz)
47 (Map) Forum for Urban Design
(Images) courtesy of Friends of the Queensway
49 (Images) dlandstudio
51 (Image) Difei Ma and Miao Yu, Flux City Studio,
Chris Reed, Coordinator and Instructor

53 (Image) Terreform ONE
55 (Images) Balmori Associates
61 (Images) Forest City Ratner Companies
63 (Image) Kohn Pedersen Fox Associates
64 (Image) Kohn Pedersen Fox Associates
69 (Images) Thomas Jost, in partnership with the Urban
Design Lab, Earth Institute of Columbia University
73 (Image) Kohn Pedersen Fox Associates
75 (Image) Forum for Urban Design
87 (Image) Forum for Urban Design
89 (Image) concept Nina Rappaport and Natalie
Jeremijenko; (Illustration) Francis Waltersdorfer
90, 91 (Images) Forum for Urban Design
93 (Image) Furman Center for Real Estate
and Urban Policy
98 (Image) courtesy of No Longer Empty
99 (Image) courtesy of New York City Department
of Parks & Recreation
101 (Images) dlandstudio
103 (Image) Forum for Urban Design
105 (Image) Hudson River Park Trust;
(Graphic) Forum for Urban Design

Unless otherwise noted, all images are the property
of the Forum for Urban Design.

The Forum for Urban Design convenes the world's preeminent leaders in architecture, urban planning, design and development—as well as professionals in government, education and journalism whose work intersects with the built environment—to discuss and debate the defining issues that face our cities.

The Forum, based in New York City, engages its fellows through programs and publications that promote awareness of contemporary urban design's best practices and greatest challenges. The Forum also publishes the Urban Design Review, a journal containing reviews of recent texts and exhibitions relevant to the field of urban design.

Board of Directors:
Daniel Rose, Chair
Alexander Garvin, President
Deborah Berke, Vice President
James Corner, Vice President
Paul Katz, Treasurer
Meredith J. Kane, Secretary
Marilyn Jordan Taylor, Immediate Past President
Daniel Brodsky
Timur Galen
Paul Goldberger
Hugh Hardy
David Haskell
Robert Yaro

Christopher Beardsley, Executive Director
Daniel McPhee, Deputy Director

This project was made possible through the support of:

CHARLIE

JUST DO BETTER NEXT TIME

4/12/12

For Lucy

I enjoyed the week-end
with you & George
My Best,
Charlie

CHARLIE

Just Do Better Next Time

A Memoir of My Mother, Addie Loudermilk

How One Woman's Unconditional Love,
Courage, and Fierce Determination
Carried Me to Success

By Charlie Loudermilk
with Vincent Coppola

Shock Design Books
454 Hamilton Street, SE, #12
Atlanta, GA 30316
www.shockdesignbooks.com

© 2011 R. Charles Loudermilk. All rights reserved. No part of this book may be reproduced in any form or by any means without the prior written permission of the Publisher, excepting brief quotations used in conjuction with reviews that are written specifically for inclusion in a newspaper or magazine.

Designed and produced by Laurie Shock
Edited by Amy Bauman

Picture credits:
Unless otherwise noted, images are courtesy of the Loudermilk family archives. Pgs. 67, 74–75 Halberstadt Studios; Pgs. ix, 116, 133, 143 © Billy Howard; Pgs. 7, 19 Courtesy of the Georgia Archives, Vanishing Georgia Collection; Pg. xiii © Gittings Portraiture; Pg. 114 © Kelly LaDuke; Pg. 89 Library of Congress; Pgs. 8, 16, 33 Courtesy of Rebecca Dale Loudermilk; Pgs. 39, 42–43, 47 Courtesy of the Orr family; Pgs. 113, 137 © 2005 Lance Davies; Pg. 131 © Joseph Duke.

First Edition
Printed in China
Library of Congress Number: 2010941691
ISBN 13: 978-0-9824779-2-2
ISBN 10: 0-9824779-2-9

Although every effort has been made to ensure the accuracy of information and credits in this book, errors are possible. Should an error or omission be found, please notify us so that we may update our records and correct the information in future editions.

Dedicated

to my grandchildren

Charlie, Chappell, Coley,

Katherine, and Robert

Contents

Introduction — Andrew Young / viii

Prologue / xi

Part One — My Mother's Son / 1

Part Two — Family Values / 78

Part Three — Building a Business / 94

Timeline / 144

INTRODUCTION

Charlie Loudermilk is passing out secrets—secrets of a successful business, family, and a lifetime of community service.

The secret is in the title, but it's hard to imagine modern mothers with such uncompromising confidence in themselves and their children to realize that children, like plants, grow in their own space and time, and in their own way.

Today's parents are driven by test scores, grades, and college cut-off dates for acceptance. But reading this memoir lets you see that Charlie's progress from struggle to success was seemingly preordained. Charlie's success doesn't come from the schools and colleges he attended, but by the confidence, prayers, and unconditional love of "Miz Addie" and the work ethic of his father Jake.

The tender-hearted, sensitive "Jeep" comes from a mother's Presbyterian sense of predestination. She need not worry, just believe, love, forgive, and keep on working. It was her faith that "this boy" has got something in him that comes from God, through "me," just like "Mary" pondered in her heart about young Jesus.

But fathers never get their due because when you're poor, work hard, and "get no respect," whether you're white or black, you develop a hard emotional shell to protect yourself from the injustices and indignity that you must suffer to survive. The shell that keeps the hurt out, also keeps the love buried deep inside. It's the fear that if you ever show or speak any love or tenderness you couldn't get yourself up in the middle of the night and work long hours to keep the city's lights on. A father's love is demonstrated by that sense of duty and responsibility that never takes a sick day.

You can't climb poles and string power lines 16–20 hours a day without pain. But there were no shots and pills, only a sip of "moonshine" for medicinal purposes, and the pride you bury inside when you paid the family grocery bill and then collapsed on the porch to stare at the stars and wonder about a God that let life be so hard that "poor folk did all the work but never got the credit or appreciation or even respect."

This is where Charlie's work ethic comes from, and where the mutual respect of Aaron's associates and customers comes from—they are friends and not numbers.

Charlie, Just do Better Next Time should be read by today's parents, so that they might see the strength of family faith, hard work, determination, and confidence in creating a future through tough times.

We must "cool out," take some of the pressure off ourselves, and say to our children, our partners, our associates, and ourselves, "Just do better next time."

It's a simple loving, faithful way to raise a family, build a business, or just live a wonderful life.

Charlie didn't just build a successful company, he made a difference in his community. When it comes to the city of Atlanta and Aaron's, Charlie really began to blossom and the city started to boom. Atlanta was blessed with a cluster of urban patriots.

By 1960 it was evident that race could pull the American South apart. Atlanta's leadership, black or white, stepped up and was determined to keep the ship of state afloat and surging full speed ahead.

Charlie, Herman Russell, Jesse Hill, and John Portman formed a nucleus of young businessmen who were willing to step forward with Mayor Ivan Allen and Coca Cola's J. Paul Austin.

There were others, but Charlie, Jesse, Portman, and Russell formed a "fearsome foursome" that were quietly ready to commit their dreams to a glorious future for Atlanta and the region. The rest is history.

The Atlanta Chamber of Commerce and a remarkable succession of Atlanta mayors created racial harmony through shared prosperity. The business-political, bi-racial partnership has kept Atlanta moving forward and Charlie's company, Aaron's, was not only first in the phonebook, but first in community involvement.

I'm sure that somewhere in the Great Beyond Jake and Miz Addie are grinning proudly "Well done, good and faithful servant. We are proud of our son."

PROLOGUE

"Never seen a guy who likes to change things as much as you do, Mr. Loudermilk."

—JERRY CREEL

I turned eighty a few years back, a milestone on a long journey. I've lived well past my biblical portion of three score and ten years, beyond even those hearty men blessed to see four score. I've lived my life in the present and rarely took time to look back. I was too busy building my business, watching my children and grandchildren blossom, and helping my hometown mature into a vital and vibrant city. I was always anticipating what was beyond the next bend in the road. But when you get to be my age, you start to think back a lot more than you think forward. You count your blessings. I've been blessed with a loving family, lifelong friends, robust health, and a successful company founded a long time ago on a shoestring. Most amazing, I've been blessed with the means and desire to change things for the better while I still can.

I've had a near perfect life, though, like most mortals, I'm an imperfect person.

I've lived the dream and wouldn't change a thing, though I hate to think that there's not a hell of lot of years until I'll be out of here and my work will be done.

Work is the engine that has driven what success I've had and whatever good I've accomplished. I was an entrepreneur long before I'd ever heard the word. I worked from the moment I was able to deliver a newspaper or haul a sack of groceries down Howell Mill Road. All these years later, I'm still working. If I notice a stone blocking a creek on my farm, I've got to move it. Don't ask me why. I'm just addicted to work. Preachers like to say they've never met a man, who on his deathbed, regretted that he did not spend more time at the office. I might be that man.

But this is not that book. Nor is it my story. In the pages that follow, I revisit what I've learned about moral values, character, determination, decency, hard work, and love of family. I leave the preaching to the preachers. I tell it like I've lived it: day by day, hurdle by hurdle, through the people I've met, in the things I've seen and tasted and struggled after my whole life. Such lessons are more valuable a legacy than material success or the buildings and philanthropic outreaches that bear my name. In my life, every one of these virtues was embodied in one person. This book is a memorial to her and the incalculable impact of her kindness and love.

We all try to understand the individuals and events that shape our lives. It's natural, whether in rousing success or bitter disappointment, to ask the question, "Why me?" Over the years, I've met men and women who were born with every advantage, and others who've had to scuffle for every crumb, every possibility, every scarce opportunity that came their way. Often, those born with silver spoons fared worse than those forced to struggle. They were worse off: less happy, unfulfilled, even despairing. I'm not recommending poverty, but material advantage does not translate directly into happiness.

As an adolescent, I struggled with the burden of shame and inferiority—my lack of the social graces as painful as my ill-fitting shoes—that accompanies every outsider trying to struggle up in life. I disguised my insecurity behind a willing smile, quick fists, and a willingness to work hard.

All these years later, "Why me?" becomes "How did the kid in the baggy overalls, living on the wrong end of the Howell Mill Road streetcar line, become the founder and chairman of a $3 billion dollar public company?"

The answer is obvious, but it has taken me a lifetime to fully appreciate it. It is embodied in a thousand unspoken sacrifices that come flooding back like the tide in a coastal marsh . . . in a thousand mornings before the sun rose when the wind whistled through the floors of our uninsulated house; in one woman's ferocious courage, stubbornness, pride, and determination that her sons would shine, prosper, and succeed and that nothing would stand in their way.

I've been told many times that I'm a person who doesn't show a lot of emotion. I despise fakeness and histrionics. I've always said, "Judge me by my actions." In this book, I struggle to cast aside the stones dammed up inside me for so many years and tap the wellspring of feeling I've never been able to express.

Addie Pinkard Loudermilk was my mother. She died in 1996. She was ninety-six years old. And this is her story.

Charlie Loudermilk

PART ONE
MY MOTHER'S SON

Chapter One

"The hustle and bustle of nascent capitalism, of big dreams being mapped out by ambitious kids in crowded schoolyards."
—Charlie Loudermilk

A special energy pulses through working class neighborhoods. There's an urgency to get to work; to shoo the kids off to school; to open the service station, corner grocery, or hot dog stand for business; to get things moving because time and money are short and every customer is important. I recall lots of clatter—the rumble of delivery trucks, the whoosh of air brakes from the school bus, children's shouts, the tinkering of someone fixing a car, the jangling of the iceman's bell as he approaches, the junkman's clatter as he made his rounds collecting scrap metal and bottles. To me, this is the sound of becoming—the music of possibility and change. To a working class boy eager to get on with life, this energy is more familiar and reassuring than birdsong or the muted whisper of sprinklers on an emerald lawn.

We know this world from books and movies. The calendar usually marks the years somewhere between the Great Depression and World War II—my childhood and adolescence—but it's timeless. You can see it today, still vibrant and vital, in immigrant neighborhoods where each night children huddle over schoolbooks at the kitchen table, where day laborers "shape up" at dawn, and where extended family members—once called cousins, uncles, and aunts—pitch in scant resources to open a café, a convenience store, a dry cleaner, or maybe a corner fruit stand. The soundtrack is the hustle and bustle of nascent capitalism, of big dreams being mapped out by ambitious kids in crowded schoolyards, and of future fortunes seeded in the tinkle of pennies exchanged for Coca-Cola bottles or errands run.

If you look closely, a woman is usually the driving force behind this unspooling success. She is the whisperer of hope, builder of confidence, wellspring of unconditional love. Fathers are alpha males, too

Opposite: A young ambitious Charlie Loudermilk—his whole life ahead of him.

often incapable of expanding or imagining their lives beyond the first person. Mothers either defer their own dreams or transform them. They struggle to nurture and protect their cubs, make sacrifices for them, and deny self-interest to assure their children's success. I see these sacrifices every day at Aaron's, my company, where so many women, often single mothers, struggle through 15- to 18-hour days, racing between job, kids, laundry, and packing lunches as the clock ticks away, compressing their lives and draining their youth.

My mother was such a woman. Rather than fading over time, my memories of her have become ever more vibrant and alive. Through this mirror, I'm carried back to my childhood and my old neighborhood—a jumble of frame houses, grocery stores, service stations, barbershops, and a hardware store, all centered around the streetcar stop on the corner of Howell Mill Road and Defoor Avenue. I see my mother up long before dawn checking to be sure that my brother Jim and I had clean clothes and breakfast to eat before slipping out the door headed for work while we dreamed the expansive dreams—I was going to be the president of the United States, and Jim wanted to be a pilot—that she'd carefully planted in our innocent hearts.

Growing up, I don't remember another mother who held a job outside the home. A woman's place was to cook and clean, raise the kids, and keep her husband content. My mother never stopped working, and my dad, Jake Loudermilk, never stopped resenting it.

In the 1930s, Atlanta women were not encouraged to stand up for themselves, and they certainly did not challenge the powers-that-be. But when Addie Loudermilk was elected president of the local PTA, that's exactly what she did; she organized the other mothers to march downtown and demand that Fulton County run long-overdue sewer lines to Evan P. Howell, my grammar school, and the rest of the neighborhood—an act that allowed us the dignity of foregoing the dank outhouse in our backyard.

Instead of supporting her, some of our neighbors may have regarded Mother as an oddball, though she was modest, openhearted and upstanding in all things, and a church-going, Jesus-loving Presbyterian. If an unkind whisper or cutting remark stung her, she never let on. Her world was as transparent and self-contained as one of those glass snow globes you find at souvenir shops—and Jim and I were at its center.

Addie Pinkard was born on the cusp of a new century. The year she was born, the Coca-Cola Bottling Company opened its first plant on Edgewood Avenue—the initial step in a commercial empire that would circle the globe. In 1900, Atlanta was still very much a railroad town. In fact, in the 1830s, the city called itself "Terminus."

Addie was quite attractive with dark wavy hair, startling blue eyes, and what my daughter Linda recalls as "a laughing, knowing look." The daughter of a railroad foreman, she was one of three children who grew up off Piedmont Road in a house the company provided supervisors to assure they were on the job 24/7. These were called "shotgun houses" because you could fire a scattergun at the front door and not hit anything but the back porch. The kitchen, living room, and bedrooms were off a hallway that ran the length of the house. I imagine Addie, neat as a pin throughout her life, growing up under clouds of embers and dust amidst the clank and rattle of the freights. With Buckhead and the leafy environs of Garden Hills literally on the other side of the tracks, I can see her, even as a young girl, dreaming about escaping.

Her father, Jack Pinkard was an upstanding man who neither drank nor smoked, which was unusual for a railroad worker even in Bible Belt Georgia. Her mother was a fragile woman who suffered a mental collapse after the birth of a second daughter, Mary. Back then, mental health care was inexact and uncertain whether you were the child of millionaire Joseph Kennedy—whose depressed, twenty-three-year-old daughter, Rosemary, endured a devastating lobotomy—or the wife of a railroad worker. My grandmother's condition deteriorated, and she was committed to what was then the Georgia State Sanitarium in Milledgeville where she remained for the rest of her life. Whatever dreams young Addie was nurturing had to be put on hold: she had a brother, Durrell, and a headstrong younger sister to look after, and later, a stepmother, my Great-"Aunt Ida."

Years later, when Ida developed diabetes, insulin was not readily available. Barely out of her teens, Addie took it upon herself to ride a streetcar to Emory University Hospital for advice on how to manage her stepmother's illness. Addie's hunger to learn was such that she developed a lifelong interest in nutrition and healthy foods that would open the door to future opportunities. One of them would change my life dramatically.

Addie's father, Jack Pinkard, and his second wife, the beloved "Aunt Ida," on the front porch of their home.

By high school, the pattern of hard work, family obligation, and fierce commitment to education that would define my mother was already established. She got up every morning before the sun, fixed breakfast, cleaned up the house, dressed, and got her kid sister, Mary, ready for school. Then she took a train, most likely the Atlantic Coast Line or the Louisville & Nashville—a schoolgirl among the businessmen—downtown to Union Station on Central Avenue and walked over to the new Fulton High School. Enrollment at the time was 140 students. She would have eaten lunch in the school cafeteria—the first to operate in an Atlanta public school—an experience that made a decided impression on her. Family records are not clear on this, but in 1917, Addie Pinkard may well have been part of Fulton High School's first graduating class of five students—all girls. Even then, graduation rates were woefully low and hovered at about 10 percent well into the 1930s. But we do know that she graduated, which was a tremendous achievement. A high school diploma back then was equivalent to today's college degree.

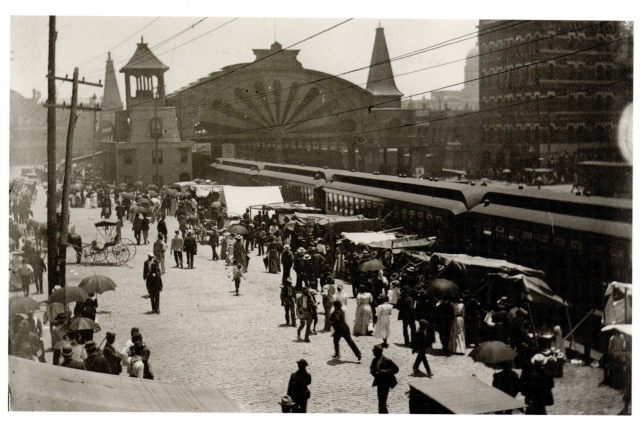
As a young girl, Addie would ride the train to a very busy Union Station in Atlanta and walk to Fulton High School.

In the first decades of the twentieth century, Atlanta's population grew to approximately 175,000, the result of the great rural migration into the cities underway all over the nation. Cities were where you found jobs and opportunities; there you could re-invent yourself, pursue your dreams, or lose yourself. In these years, 33 percent of Atlanta's residents were African-American, an early indication that the city with its traditionally black colleges and bustling Sweet Auburn business district would become a "Black Mecca," home to civil rights leaders like Martin Luther King Jr., Ralph David Abernathy, and Andrew Young.

We all remember momentous events that unfolded during our childhood and adolescence. As I've said, my youthful memories are certainly more vivid than today's day-to-day occurrences. They reflect the people, events, and things that shaped me, providing the background music of my life.

As an adolescent living in Atlanta, my mother probably would have been aware of the excitement of a nine-year-old named Robert "Bobby" Jones winning the city's junior golf championship, maybe of the opening of the magnificent Winecoff Hotel on Peachtree Street, and certainly of the murder of

The Loudermilk-Hazel Creek Grist Mill near Demorest, Georgia in Habersham County—Jake's hometown.

Mary Phagan, a thirteen-year-old employee at the National Pencil Factory. Addie and Mary Phagan were the same age. Leo Frank, the factory manager, was arrested in a sensational case that still draws national attention. Frank was convicted, imprisoned, and later lynched by an anti-Semitic mob in Marietta. He would be pardoned seventy years later. But she probably wouldn't have been aware that Asa Candler sold the Coca-Cola Company to a group led by Robert Woodruff for the seemingly staggering sum of $25 million, one of the best bargains in history.

    My father, Jake, and his siblings were among those making their way to the big city from the rocky and inhospitable soil of Habersham County in northeast Georgia. Today, those mountains are prime resort real estate; back then, they were little more than a physical and psychological extension of Appalachia, with few jobs, pitiable schools, and scant infrastructure. Their poverty was such that my father remembered a diet that often was nothing more than cornmeal and sorghum syrup. His father, my grandfather, a big rawboned man of German stock, was an alcoholic who would disappear for days on end, leaving his wife and many children to fend for themselves.

Jake Loudermilk left Demorest and joined the army—the first rung up the economic ladder for millions of impoverished Americans. The United States had entered World War I in April 1917, two years after the Germans torpedoed the ocean liner *Lusitania*. The sinking of the ship, which was heading out of New York bound for Liverpool with 1,959 people on board, began the drumbeat for war. In boot camp, Jake developed medical issues, by his account a severe allergic reaction to army rations, and was issued an honorable discharge.

At the time, the electrification of Atlanta was expanding beyond the streetcars and downtown business district. The Georgia Railway and Power Company (a predecessor to Georgia Power) needed tough men willing to handle the dangerous and exhausting job of stringing power lines in the treetops. My father and his brothers who could barely read and write, leaped at the opportunity for a steady paycheck.

My father would remain at Georgia Power for forty-five years, rising from lineman to crew foreman. And there, Jake Loudermilk's ambitions ended. Poverty makes people risk averse. My father was happy to remain a salary man, put in his forty hours, draw his paycheck, go home, have dinner, and while away the hours with his buddies on the street corner. He didn't see the need for his two sons to aspire to anything beyond a high school diploma and a steady job. He was straight and honest. He could not bear to owe any man a dime. If he did, his coworkers used to joke, he'd follow you home to pay you back. In many ways, he was a hard man. I believe he loved me, but in my whole life, he never hugged me, put his hand on my shoulder, or paid me a compliment, though I ached for his touch and lived for his praise.

Without question, he reflected the attitudes of his time. He didn't like black people (he said there was just one African-American living in Habersham County where he grew up), and he distrusted Jews except for a man named Moskins, whom he loved, who sold clothes on Decatur Street. When my father showed up once or twice a year to purchase work clothes, Mr. Moskins, he said, always treated him with "respect." Jake was not envious of wealthy people, but he felt they inhabited a world that was, by definition, closed to him.

My father also had more than his share of charisma. The men on his crew admired and respected him; women claimed Jake "had a twinkle in his eye."

If he did, it was never there for me.

How such seeming opposites as my parents met, courted, married, and spent most of their lives together is still peculiar to me. Upon first meeting, young Addie with her dark wavy hair, blue eyes, and confident personality, certainly would have drawn twinkly-eyed Jake like a magnet. But beyond that, in so many ways, they were worlds apart. The deeper question—the one I wrestle with—is how this volatile mix of motherly devotion and fatherly indifference; of determination and complacency; of self-sacrifice and self-absorption; and of great hope and meager ambition, become the crucible in which the child I was became the man I am.

And sometimes, late at night when the business of daily life is winding down, I wonder how the father I have been has shaped the lives and dreams of my own son and daughters and, through the powerful and often unconscious chain of connection that is a family, my grandchildren and beyond.

My mother inspired me to attain what success I've had. She did it by good example and encouragement—and without a harsh word or criticism that I can recall. Today, hers would be called unconditional love. And yet, I confess, it was my father I was always trying to please; it was his praise I constantly sought, an impossible quest that has kept me chasing his shadow all these years.

The charismatic Jake Loudermilk—twinkly-eyed, but emotionally elusive with his children.

Chapter Two

"Why can't I be president?
My mother said I could be president!"
—Charlie "Jeep" Loudermilk

On Howell Mill Road, everyone called me "Jeep." The nickname had nothing to do with the rugged "government purpose" four-wheel drive vehicle that carried GIs off to Europe and the Pacific theaters in World War II (I'm older than that Jeep); I was named for "Eugene the Jeep," a character in the old *Popeye* comics. Jeep looked like a yellow dog, walked on his hind legs and ate nothing but orchids. He had unique powers, could teleport himself, was highly intelligent, and was able to solve complex problems.

The one problem I remember solving made me a favorite with the men who hung around the auto repair shop on Howell Mill Road. I was walking down the street one morning when one of the guys shouted, "Charlie, what's the number?"

Somehow, I came up with the three-number combination that won the "Bug" that night. And from that moment, I was christened "Jeep." The Bug was essentially an illegal version of today's Georgia Lottery. To win, you had to guess the last three numbers of that day's New York Stock Exchange's trading volume, a figure beyond reproach since it was published in the newspapers. (In New York City, bookies use the last three figures of the daily "handle," the total amount of money bet that day at one of the area racetracks.) Back then, you could bet a penny on the Bug and win $5. Hit for a nickel, the return was $25, less 10 percent for the "runner" who took your bet. Keep in mind, $25 was more than a week's pay for most men. The Bug was run by Raymond Parks, who, among other things, operated a cigarette vending business. I believe Raymond is still alive today.

Seventy years later, the old timers still call me "Jeep" because of that lucky guess, but there's more to it than that. To have the men who made-up the local pecking order—whether mechanics working on bootleggers' souped-up cars, memorable characters like grocer Bill Springer, or layabouts on the

A young Charlie Loudermilk, eager to become anything he wanted to, even president.

corner—confer a nickname on me was a big deal. Why did they include me in the first place and not some other kid?

I was the kind of kid who got along with everyone. I was curious and respectful, happy to run an errand or to pitch-in when something needed doing, able to take an interest in a grown-up conversation. Years later, these "people skills" would often be the difference between failure and success.

But I was a regular kid, too, playing baseball and football, rolling cigarettes made out of a noxious weed we called "rabbit tobacco," and trying to figure what girls were all about. Back then, we could entertain ourselves with a hoop and a stick. Like millions of other Depression-era boys and girls, I listened to *Little Orphan Annie* on the radio in the evenings and sent in my Ovaltine proof-of-purchase label and was rewarded with a "secret decoder" that arrived in the mail a few weeks later. I'd use it to decode "secret messages" broadcast during the radio show.

On Sunday nights, Mother prepared the treat of the week for my father, my brother, and me: a hearty oyster stew. Oysters came in a wooden barrel. She'd mix them with milk and peppers and flour. It was cheap, easy to make, and really good. Sometimes, I can still taste it.

Howell Mill Road was my whole world, and I wanted to be as much a part of it as my father, who spent his free time on the corner with his friends. Everything beyond Springer's Grocery, Crane's Hot Dog Stand, Couey's Barbershop, and the cluster of services stations and other small businesses at the Defoor Avenue intersection was strange and intimidating. Buckhead? The rich neighborhood was as distant as the stars.

Defoor Avenue was "the crooked road." We lived a block north off Howell Mill Road, in my late Grandfather Pinkard's wood-frame house. At the time, 11 White Street was jointly owned by my mother, and her brother and sister; neither of her siblings ever demanded a penny's rent.

My brother, Jim, was four years older and less outgoing than I. Mechanical-minded as a kid, he was already a miniature of the aeronautical engineer he'd become. Like most big brothers, he could be a bully. I remember the day we were finally getting indoor plumbing, well, actually, we were getting a toilet framed in a corner of the back porch. I was in the yard watching the plumber running the pipes under the house. Jim and my cousin Vernon Yates were there, and, in that needless cruelty so typical of older boys, they began berating me, calling me a "dumb little kid," this, that, and the other. I recall the plumber crawling out from under the house like The Phantom come to my rescue.

"Wait a minute, boys," he drawled. "I don't see any blue ribbons on your chests."

That crawl space under the house was my hiding place, my fortress of solitude. I'd spend hours there daydreaming about how I was going to grow up and become a millionaire. Back then, a millionaire was a very big deal; in my mind, it put you in a class with Henry Ford, the Rockefellers, and the Carnegies.

At the time, three sisters, Gladys, Doris, and Margie Robinson lived next door. One day, a bunch of us got into that familiar kids' conversation, "What are you going to be when you grow up?" Everybody was talking at once, and I forgot myself and piped up.

"I'll be president!"

Everyone laughed. My feelings were badly hurt, and I demanded, "Why can't I be president? Mother said I could be president!" It became this big joke. Long after everyone went home, I kept ask-

Charlie's childhood home where the crawl space become his haven to dream of becoming a millionaire.

ing myself: "Why shouldn't I be president of the United States? Never heard I couldn't."

Looking back, I see that even as a small boy I was already looking beyond the possible and familiar and past the circumscribed boundaries of my father's life. I was chasing something more without knowing exactly what it was or when to stop. Mother always told me, "Charlie, if you are willing to pay the price, you can be anything you want."

Life has a way of grinding down a person's dreams, particularly if he or she is trying to struggle up the socioeconomic ladder. You want to be in on things, but you don't know how to go about it. Positive role models and mentors are hard to come by on street corners. So you flounder and figure out things as best you can. You put your head down and bull forward.

Unless you're careful though, you can build dreams around unrealistic expectations: overnight success, public adulation, effortless mastery of the game or one's competition. Careers in business, medicine, law, engineering, and sales, are certainly attainable, but they demand relentless preparation and hard work. Accordingly, they are often ruled out as too steep a climb. Without drive and determination, the entrepreneurial spirit can wither. For me, "overnight success" translated to many years of hard work, including many evenings where—too wound up to sleep—I reviewed never-ending lists of things to do and worried about financing, unpaid invoices, and underutilized inventory.

The amazing thing is my dreams came true. I never did run for president, but everything else yielded to my mother's dictum about "paying the price." I willingly paid the price, but so did the people around me. Success does not come without sacrifice or cost to those who care about you.

I suspect young Addie Pinkard was the dreamer among her siblings. As fate would have it, it was her brother, Durrell, who wound up living a Buckhead lifestyle. Addie must have brushed her vain, younger sister Mary's hair a thousand times, and it was Mary who married the carpet merchant—Henry Surgeon—who swept her off to New York City like a princess in the *Arabian Nights*. My mother landed on White Street with an indifferent husband, two rambunctious boys, and an outdoor toilet.

Lucybelle Loudermilk was Charlie's aunt, an old maid who lived with them for many years at 11 White Street.

My father's unmarried sister, Lucybelle, a formidable figure at Rich's Department Store for half-a-century, lived in our front bedroom for many years; other assorted uncles and aunts and my alcoholic grandfather showed up occasionally. My father loved his mother but did not care for his father, who'd basically abandoned his family for moonshine whiskey. To me, Grandfather Loudermilk was charming. I remember visiting him up in Demorest, Georgia, where we'd sit on the porch set just back a few yards from the turtleback road going up to Lake Burton and Lake Rabun. Even then, only rich people from

Atlanta had lots up there. I'd watch these long cars driving by and say to myself, "I'm going to get me one of those one day."

———•———

When Grandmother Loudermilk was diagnosed with a necrotic cancer, it was my mother who cared for her. Her own sons and daughters were unwilling to take on the burden. I used to ask myself how my grandmother's flesh-and-blood children could allow a daughter-in-law to bear such a terrible responsibility. (I found the odor of my grandmother's decaying flesh overwhelming.) They simply knew she wouldn't refuse, an answer that not only reveals my mother's kindness and generous spirit but my own blindness. A time would come when I would be similarly tested and found wanting.

To care for my grandmother, Mother gave up a good job in an Atlanta public school cafeteria on Forrest Avenue behind the Sears & Roebuck on Ponce de Leon Avenue. At the time, my future friend and renowned architect, John Portman, was a student there. My mother was ahead of her time in that she understood that fresh fruits and vegetables were vital to every child's health. She would have been horrified at the junk food and epidemic obesity everywhere today. She served 5-cent lunches, made possible because of federal government subsidies of powdered milk, flour, cheese, beans, peas, and other staples. The bureaucracies made it almost impossible to transfer from one school to another, so she found work at a Fulton County elementary school that was closer to home

All these years later, with both my parents deceased, I find it ironic, and more than a little painful, that my father never stopped comparing my mother to his own. And always found her lacking.

Such nuances, of course, were lost on me at the time. I was the "Jeep," rushing around the streets and bursting with energy and enthusiasm, my uncertainties about the world that stretched beyond Howell Mill Road buried for the moment. One of the joys of living in a working-class area is an excess—even an overload—of stimulation. Much of life in such an area is lived in the street rather than behind closed doors. An endless number of empty lots, creeks, school yards, and abandoned buildings were ours to play in and explore; clanking trains and trolleys, street-corner prophets, drunks, drifters, and hoboes making their way up from the railroad tracks that cut through our neighborhood were our distractions. I could scavenge all sorts of materials: lumber and crates for tree houses and scooters, sand and scrap metal, tires, broken clocks. It was a feast for a boy's imagination.

One year, I built a pond in our backyard after finding the cement I needed in an abandoned warehouse in a Fulton County park. Broken bags were scattered on the floor. I went home and got my wagon. I filled it up with the stuff, got some sand and dug a hole, and lined the sides and bottom with cement. When it hardened, I went down to one of the tributaries of Peachtree Creek and seined fish to stock it. My pond wasn't very deep. Back then, the weather seemed a hell of a lot colder than it is now. The water would freeze with the fish in it. When it thawed, the fish would come back to life and swim away. Who knew fish could live after being frozen in ice?

When I look back at the freedom I enjoyed and then at my own grandchildren today . . . at the idea of a kid roaming through abandoned buildings and empty lots—not to mention mixing concrete in the backyard without his parents' permission or intervention—I'm both astounded and saddened. Life then was upfront and open, sometimes literally. Our house never had a front- or backdoor key. And Mother fed anyone who showed up hungry at our backdoor. In this, my father, who'd known hunger and poverty as a boy, encouraged her. A stranger might be a good person who'd simply fallen on hard times or a friend you hadn't yet met. During the Depression, millions of such people were on the move. The world has changed dramatically and not for the better.

The front porch was where families and friends gathered to try to resolve problems, work out grievances or settle arguments. We didn't know what a psychiatrist was.

Hiding in the tangled weeds and underbrush near that same creek I'd seined, I watched the Ku Klux Klan drag one of our neighbors, a drunk who neglected his family, and beat the hell out of him. Most people don't know that the Ku Klux Klan was reconstituted in Atlanta in 1915. And after World War I, the organization's ranks soared to as many as six million members, many in Indiana and other states outside the South. Hugo Black, who later became a U.S. Supreme Court justice, was a Klansman. And the Klan got a big boost from the film *Birth of a Nation* (1915), in which Hollywood director D.W. Griffith depicted Klansmen as noble knights riding to the rescue of the poor and downtrodden.

On Howell Mill Road, the Kluxers served this quasi-police function in the white community, enforcing their own brand of morality. When the punishment ended, I watched the Klansmen burn a cross—in the middle of the city less than a mile from my house—standing in a solemn circle. Since most of the hooded and sheeted men were neighbors, I wondered why the victim didn't recognize their voices. Today, I think he probably did.

The neighborhood had a strong religious feeling to it. Most of us were Methodists or Southern Baptists. Mother regularly went to church and made sure Jim and I were right there beside her. I don't recall my father stepping inside a church door except for my and Jim's wedding days. A few times a year, the tent preachers passed through town. They'd put up a big tent back on Howell Mill Road, scatter sawdust on the ground, set up their folding chairs and benches, tune up their guitars and fiddles, do their preaching, and take up their collections.

At these revivals, I'd stand outside the tent listening. The Jesus-loving, devil-hating preachers would really put the fear of the Lord in folks with all that hell and damnation, fire and brimstone. The music would build and build, and then the testifying would begin. Soon, many in the congregation would begin speaking in tongues and holy-rolling, and then they'd rush up front to confess their sins, accept Jesus, and be saved.

The Ku Klux Klan maintained a strong presence in Charlie's neighborhood and all over the South as he was growing up.

I remember sitting at our little breakfast room table after one of the revivals. Mother had gone to work already, and I was getting ready for school. A beam of light appeared out of nowhere. I sat there for a long time transfixed. I knew the Good Lord was telling me some stuff. The truth is, I've never been comfortable expressing any emotion out loud, be it personal or religious. I feel it; I'm just not about to shout it.

Chapter Three

"The joy of change in my pocket was magical."
—Charlie Loudermilk

Work flows through my life like a river, carrying me forward in time and back to my earliest memories of my mother. When I was a boy, very few women worked outside the home no matter how dire the family situation. But my mother always worked. Job piled upon job, in cafeterias and restaurant kitchens, a mountain of work that she climbed without complaint until her legs literally gave out on her. Given this work ethic, it is no surprise that hustling for a buck came naturally to me. The jingle of change in my pocket was magical.

Back then, it was common for children to earn pocket money or pay for the bike or baseball glove their parents couldn't afford. There were always newspapers to be delivered, cars to be washed, or groceries to be sacked and carried. For a while, I sold the *Saturday Evening Post* and *Life* magazine door-to-door out of a little satchel; I also collected discarded soda bottles for the 1-cent deposit the original purchaser had paid. Anything was worth a try. One summer, I grew mint for a lady in Spring Lake Park who had a business that involved blending fresh mint into tea leaves.

My father and his Georgia Power crew spent a lot of time replacing rotting wooden poles that supported the power lines. The old poles were made of cedar. Every year, he'd bring home two or three discarded poles and leave them for me in the driveway. I'd cut them up and chop them into kindling that I'd then sell to local grocers for 10 cents a bundle; they'd charge 20 cents to their customers. Unfortunately, the blinking lights and bells of the nickel pinball machine in the back of Crane's hotdog shack mesmerized me like a snake charmer's cobra and swallowed most of my earnings.

My "rich uncle," Durrell Pinkard, operated a dry-cleaning store in Buckhead near where the Buckhead Theatre is today. Uncle Durrell, my mother's older brother, had married into a wealthy family—real estate

Opposite: Charlie's Uncle Durrell Pinkard owned a successful dry cleaning store and was wealthy enough to afford an electric refrigerator that made real ice cubes.

Charlie, with his class at Evan P. Howell School, second row from the back and third from the right.

mogul Jack Smith was his father-in-law—and inherited what seemed like half the retail space in Buckhead. He was so rich that he had an electric refrigerator that made ice cubes. I loved the taste of a homemade ice cube. He and my Aunt Elizabeth were the most generous people I knew. Every year on Christmas Eve, they'd stop by our house and shower Jim and me with holiday cheer and the gift-wrapped presents my parents couldn't afford to buy.

Uncle Durrell was so extravagant that my father, who'd salt away his meager earnings like a squirrel in autumn, actually refused to attend the big parties he'd throw on the principle that he "wouldn't help him spend his money." Durrell would grill thick steaks and serve bourbon and good scotch whiskey, inviting all his neighbors and friends. Ironically, my old man was right. Uncle Durrell wound up broke and despondent. Mother and I gave him money to pay bills and did our best to try to keep him afloat, but at the time we were struggling ourselves.

When I was a boy, Mother helped out at Pinkard's dry cleaners on Saturdays—it was one of her many jobs—and I tagged along. Once a year, she'd go through the piles of unclaimed clothes. Durrell told her she was welcome to take anything that had been there for more than a year. So Jim and I often wore handoffs, but they were damned good handoffs because rich folks had left them there. Soon enough, my cousin, Lee Pinkard, and I started our own business: we'd sell bottles of Coca-Cola for 5 cents from a sidewalk stand in front of Pinkard's to passersby. Since we paid 80 cents for a case of twenty-four bottles to start, we were selling the soda at a nearly 40 percent markup. When we cleared out our inventory for the day, we'd split our profit and head over to the Buckhead Theatre. There we'd spend the afternoon a million miles from Atlanta, transported by the cartoons, the increasingly grim newsreels—Hitler was on the rise—and the double features. That little soda stand forged a direct connection between work and the fruits (candy) of my labor. If you're reading this, you may know that I bought that theater, at one time called the Roxy, and recently completed restoring my childhood pleasure palace to its former glory complete with its original name, the Buckhead Theatre—not for me, but for future generations of dreamers and escape artists.

The soda stand confirmed something I was learning about myself: Not only was I willing to work, but I *liked* working, particularly when it brought me into contact with people. Today, I'm convinced that the experiences and people skills I picked up as a boy are the biggest factor in my success; they gave me a tremendous advantage when I began my career. I'd come across people I never would have met had I grown up in a sheltered family or gone to school in an ivory tower. Everyone had something to teach me; sometimes it was positive, other times it was negative, sometimes it was both. Very little in life is black and white; most things are nuanced and shaded.

When I was twelve or thirteen years old, I worked for Mr. Bates who ran a combination grocery, feed, and hardware store on our corner. (I'd actually helped *build* the store, throwing bricks up to the two masons working on a scaffold. I tossed a lot of bricks for just a couple of dollars.) Bates had a son a few years older than I; we worked together on Friday afternoons and all day Saturday. I'd get so damned tired—the store didn't close until 10 PM. on Saturday night—that I'd lie back on the feed sacks and fall asleep. On Sunday mornings, my legs would ache because I'd worked so much.

One day, the owner's son and I were in the back of the store stacking stove pipe. The pipe came in sections that you had to put together into a chimney. He'd throw the tin sections to me, and I'd stack it on the shelves. On one toss, I caught a piece of the pipe the wrong way, and it cut my thumb deeply. I ran over to the office of the neighborhood doctor, which, as I recall, was no bigger than a closet and was located behind the barber shop! Given the man's lack of skill and affinity for whiskey, a closet was probably too expansive a space. I don't know what he did, but all these years later my left thumb is still numb. But in those days, malpractice didn't exist.

I grew up in the teeth of the Great Depression. No one had a car, so the neighborhood women walked to the store or, if the family had a telephone, they called in a weekly order. Mr. Bates had a driver to make deliveries. The driver and I would don our white coats and make deliveries on Friday afternoons and all day Saturday. The thing was this: I could read, but the driver couldn't. He worked for practically nothing; I worked for 50 cents on those long Friday afternoons and for a dollar on Saturday.

The deliveries were all cash money, no checks or credit cards. I'd collect the receipts and make change. When we were through, we'd come back to the grocery and check out with Mr. Bates. When I arrived for work one Friday afternoon and put on my coat, I found a dollar stuffed in the pocket.

"Where the heck did this come from?" I thought to myself. I'd long since turned over the money I'd collected the previous weekend, and Mr. Bates had meticulously checked it.

I pondered it some more—hell, a dollar was a good bit of money—and I decided to hold on to it. The next time my mother and Jim visited me at the store, Mr. Bates launched into a long speech. "What a hard worker Charlie is," he told them, adding, "but *he's got to be honest*." He kept going, adding this or that compliment, but always tossing in this stuff about honesty.

My mother didn't miss much. "Charlie, have you stolen anything from Mr. Bates?" she demanded as we walked home. "What is Mr. Bates talking about?"

I told her about the dollar I'd found. "Try and do better next time," she said softly. That's what she always said when I screwed up.

That damn Mister Bates had set a trap for me! I still don't know if I should have known better and handed the dollar over to him when I found it. But I knew I'd paid him every cent I'd collected. There had been no shortage. When I look back now, what he did seems a dishonest way to demonstrate the value of honesty. At the time, all I could think of was, "Why would he do that to me?"

So I went to work for Bill Springer, the other grocer. Springer was a real neighborhood character, full of fun and mischief. He ran his business out of an old wood-frame building that wasn't much more than a shanty. I'm not sure he even locked the place at night, but times were different then in a lot of ways.

The food you purchased was, well, a lot closer to its natural state. No prepackaged chickens or cuts of beef vacuum-wrapped in cellophane.

In the winter, Bill would buy fresh-killed rabbits from local farmers, eight or ten at a time. He'd hang the rabbits from a big nail on the grocery door—try to imagine this today at your local gleaming white, fluorescent-lit supermarket—and the housewives would come in and pick out their rabbits. (I figured the farmers could spot the rabbits more easily when it snowed, though I'm not sure about that.) Produce was fresh and locally grown—the very thing the "green" enthusiasts argue for today. Chickens and livestock weren't injected with growth hormones and antibiotics; they weren't slaughtered en masse and then shipped halfway across the country. You didn't hear about e. coli infections. If there was an outbreak, it was not going to travel far.

Fred Springer, Bill's brother, was the butcher. You could find him in the back of the store—sawdust scattered on the floor—standing over his butcher block cutting up half a hog. The Springers kept live poultry in a coop on the sidewalk. The ladies would come by and pick one out. After that, I'd have to "dress" them, which meant I had to kill, pluck, and gut them. I hated it.

Atlanta was still very country in those days. In my neighborhood, all the men wore overalls—for work, hanging around, whatever. I did, too. Given my diminutive size, this made me the target of one of Bill Springer's endless practical jokes. One day while I was working, he came up behind me, grabbed the back of my overalls and, before I could react, hung me on that rabbit nail. I couldn't get off. All the customers knew me and got a big kick out of Ol' Jeep hanging up there, hollering like crazy.

But the day came when Bill got nailed himself—for messing around with the druggist's wife. But this, of course, only added to his legend. Of course, this kind of stuff happens everywhere, but, as I've said, in these neighborhoods, so much of life is lived out loud and outside.

I've heard that when people get to be a certain age they tend to paint the past in a rosy glow. While that may be true of some people, I'm not naïve or overly sentimental. There was a downside to living in a bubble. When I ventured out of the neighborhood to attend high school and the fancy summer camp that would employ my mother, I developed a suffocating insecurity about my speech and manners, my hand-me-down clothes, and my worn-out shoes. Stuffing cardboard into my shoes was second nature to me. Some folks even carried around extra pieces to make on-the-fly repairs, the way cars carry spare tires. No one on Howell Mill Road would have even noticed these things.

If I felt protected and comfortable, it was because this small self-contained community was all I knew. Of course, the world would prove a much bigger and more complicated place than I'd reckoned. Isn't that what growing up is about? At the time, I was Jake Loudermilk's son and he was a salt-of-the-earth guy who commanded the respect of his peers because of his steady job and seductive personality. I was also Addie Loudermilk's son, and quietly, unobtrusively, lovingly, she struggled to breathe life and hope and happiness into my mortal clay.

Yes, the neighborhood was poor, and its residents were mostly uneducated and unsophisticated. The men on the corner could be crude and sometimes cruel. They were bored and always eager for a spectacle. As I've mentioned, I was smaller than most of the other kids, but I was wiry, strong, and eager to please. At eleven, I could pick up a 100-pound sack of feed, carry it outside, and load it into the back of a customer's pickup truck. For whatever reason, the men kept egging me and another neighborhood boy named Crafton Matthews, to prove who was the toughest.

We ended up in a knock-down, drag-out fight in front of Springer's grocery. Like two roosters, we fought while the "adults" cheered us on. Our fury was such that a conductor stopped his streetcar so his passengers could watch the spectacle. We kept on slugging each other until we were both played out. I was maybe eleven or twelve years old at the time, not really a kid anymore. In the end, I got beat up, but I think I won the fight.

My father raised fighting cocks. He called them "game chickens." The fierce, hyperaggressive birds with their glaring eyes and slashing spurs remained his passion for the rest of his life, more so than the women he was chasing. I remember he was arrested one time at a cockfight in Marietta. My mother had to bail him out. On the day he died, he still had lots of chickens, but only one wife. Mother took care of him, too.

Cockfighting has been around for thousands of years. It is bloody and messy. Jake Loudermilk would feed and train his birds as carefully as a trainer brings along a promising boxer. He'd cut off the roosters' combs and the bright red fleshy wattle under their beaks to keep opponents from grabbing on during fights, which often went to the death. He'd file down the spurs (which grow back naturally like fingernails) and tie on a set of steel spurs (gaffs), using leather leggings.

As a kid, I'd watch these furious chickens go at each other, at the last second launching their feet up at the breast or the eyes of an opponent. If a spur, sharp and curved as a needle, pierced one of the birds' heart, the match was over.

To me, the amazing thing was that my father not only knew the breeds—Allen Roundhead, Rhode Island Red, etc.—but he could instantly recognize an individual chicken among the hundreds of roosters that passed in front of him. Long after he retired to some property Mother had purchased in Sandy Springs, he'd sit there—even into his seventies—and feed those chickens. He'd study them as if they were some exotic species and sort them into different pens. It was his life.

I've always loved dogs. When I worked for Bill Springer, I had a little dog that would slip back into Fred's butcher shop, grab a bone, and race out the front door. I can't think of that darn mutt's name. One day, Bill cornered my dog and tied a paper bag with a few peas in it to his tail. At the sound of those rattling peas, the poor dog took off running down Howell Mill Road and then up the hill to our house on White Street. The house didn't have any planks or insulation between the floor and the ground, just the crawl space I've mentioned. I found my dog under there, scared to death. Every time he moved, the bag would rattle. I guess he thought it was a rattlesnake. I crawled back in there and coaxed him out. I was really furious at Bill for that.

But Bill was also capable of acts of kindness and support that made a boy feel good about himself. Hell, the money I earned wasn't anything. I just wanted to work and get something done. One of my more exotic financial ventures involved a bull calf. Back then, you could buy a calf for $3.00 when the grass was green, graze it—neighbors' backyards and parcels of vacant land made good pastures—and then, six months later ("when the grass was brown"), sell the fatted calf to the meatpackers at White Provisions for $12.00—a 400 percent return on investment.

Bill let me go up to the auction barns on Brady Avenue with his delivery man driving the panel truck. I bought a calf, which, unfortunately, I grew very attached to. I used to ride around the neighborhood on its back. I'm probably the only cowboy to ever get thrown onto a concrete sidewalk. This youthful fascination with cattle ranching continued for much of my life, and I've spent small fortunes on prize breeding bulls and cows, but I've never come close to clearing a profit again.

When I was a boy, working-class communities like ours were as tightly knit as prairie towns. Everyone knew one another, kept an eye on each other's children, and gathered in cafés and diners to hear the latest news and gossip. Those who remained took a special pride in one of their own determined to move on. You see this today, but it's usually associated with sports. Bill Springer was such a person. He'd never leave the neighborhood, but he was much more supportive of me than my own dad. As I got older, I worked with a man named Fritz Orr at his summer camp, graduated from North Fulton High School, and went into the service. Along the way, my relationship with Bill blossomed. Although men of my generation don't share these sentiments easily, I know he was proud that I was ambitious and eager to test myself. I can't rightly call him a mentor, but it really mattered to a have a strong and popular male figure encouraging me.

Years later, when I was serving in the Navy during World War II, Bill would pluck silver dollars from the grocery's cash register—two, three, or four at a time—and give them to me when I was home on leave. It doesn't sound like much, but it was. Today, I still have those precious coins. I keep them in a safety deposit box.

Chapter Four

"Addie's boys would have the same opportunities wealthy kids had. Isn't that the American Dream?"
—Charlie Loudermilk

I look a lot like my mother. As a kid, I loved being around her. But if someone dared call me a "momma's boy," fists would fly. As I grew older, like most men, I became too self-involved to understand that my world literally turned on its axis because of her. She was up with the sun and worked until after dark. Her influence was subtle and regular like the tides; quietly powerful, often unremarked. As my father's sway over his boys waned, Mother's influence grew stronger, more direct, and determined.

Mother was ambitious. She was one of a tiny minority of Atlanta women who'd finished high school. She'd studied nutrition on her own and absorbed information like a sponge. When most women were essentially second-class citizens, Mother had a need, distinct from her maternal instincts, to make good. When I ask myself what triggered my furious desire to succeed, Mother's face is right there, staring at me in the mirror.

In loving us, she often neglected herself. My daughter Linda still remembers her granny's dressing table with its ruffled skirt and creams and perfume bottles arranged in perfect order. Perfect, I now realize, because she never pampered herself. She didn't have time to be a proper lady; she was a working lady. She still had that dressing table when she was an old woman, a shrine, perhaps, to her lost and long-ago youth.

She worked seven days a week at the Davis Brothers' restaurant (today known as Davis Cafeterias) in downtown Atlanta. She worked early morning to late at night in an unbelievably hard job that paid maybe $30 a week. Much of her life, Mother suffered debilitating migraine headaches, but she worked

Opposite: Addie was driven, ambitious, and committed to success—the mirror image of her son Charlie.

right through them. You couldn't get her to see a doctor. Because of the long hours, she had to hire a lady to fix our meals and do laundry and light cleaning. Back then, you didn't pay a maid but a dollar a day and carfare. The woman, whose name was Mattie, rode the streetcar to our house every day. Doing our sad little pile of laundry, Mattie couldn't help but notice that my mother's undergarments were so ragged that she was embarrassed to hang them on the clothesline. What would the neighbors think? Although Mother wasn't worried about any of that, Mattie, bless her soul, took it upon herself to buy her employer underwear in one of the downtown shops. Of course, Mother paid her back.

When I needed a bicycle with a basket for my newspaper route, Mother went up to the Western Auto store on Peachtree and 10th Street and signed the $15.00 note. She bought the twin beds Jim and I slept on from Cobb Furniture Company on Marietta Street and paid a dollar or two for them each

Charlie and his brother Jim, above, slept on solid mahogony beds that their mother Addie worked very hard to purchase at a time when money was scarce. Charlie has them still.

week—back then, such purchases were made "on time"—out of her paycheck. Mother sweated for those beds, but she loved the fact she raised two boys who slept on "mahogany beds." Until the day she died, she'd ask me occasionally, "Where are they?"

Yup, I've still got them.

Mother rarely went to a movie. Never out to dinner. Didn't have an automobile. Didn't matter. Instead, she gave us piano lessons. Her life experiences may have been limited, but she understood the world intuitively and was trying to prepare us to meet its challenges. Her boys would have the same opportunities that wealthier kids had. Isn't that the American Dream?

Unfortunately, piano didn't take for either Jim or me. I'm the kid riding a calf down the street, hanging from a peg in my overalls, getting into fistfights. I didn't even wear underwear most of the time. So it's no surprise that I didn't like piano lessons.

The one time we did go to the movies, Mother took me to a downtown picture palace to see *The Adventures of Tom Sawyer*. I guess this would have been the 1938 version produced by David O. Selznick just before he released *Gone with the Wind*. Afterward, as we strolled out into the bright afternoon sunlight, an unexpected gloom settled over me. It seemed a sad, wistful movie. I hadn't enjoyed it and thought Mother had wasted her money. I wouldn't say that, of course, but I remember—perhaps it was the small voice of conscience—realizing that she couldn't afford to do something like this. Mostly, I didn't understand the extent of the sacrifices she was making or why. Now I do, and it breaks my heart to think that seventy years would pass before I understood the real message of *Tom Sawyer*. Today, when I go to a movie, I make sure it's not a sad one. There's enough sadness in the world. I don't have to go to a movie to see it.

You hear so much about parenting. There are flotillas of how-to books and oceans of theories. If you believe that the child is father to the man, then you become the parent you had, or perhaps, you swim against the current and end up on the opposite shore. Maybe you just muddle along. No one teaches you how to be a good father or mother. Those rare and transcendent parents flow like a gentle current guiding the lives of their children. My mother grew up without a mother and with a father who was working most of the time. She was forced to raise a sister when she was barely more than a child herself. She married a man who couldn't or wouldn't show love or affection. And yet, she was enriched rather than coarsened by her experiences.

When I did something wrong or messed up in class—and that was often—she'd always say, "Charlie, just do better next time." That was it. "*Just do better next time.*" And I knew she was with me. I still hear those words; I still see her gazing at me with a love that convinced me I could run though walls. She didn't say "I love you" over and over the way we do now with kids and friends and whomever. Mother was action more than words. At the time, I thought all this was normal; I believed all mothers were there for their sons and daughters. I devalued unconditional love. Had anyone asked, Mother probably would have defined parenting simply: Making sure your children are better off in all the things that matter than you are. Now, I tell people who've done a good job parenting, "You've *out-sired* yourself."

Chapter Five

"Everything was black or white, right or wrong. No in-betweens."
—Charlie Loudermilk

My father, Jake Loudermilk, was one of seven siblings who made their way out of the north Georgia mountains, leaving behind the poor soil, heat, hunger, and depredations of their father, a moonshiner who drank more than he could distill. Four of the brothers went to work for Georgia Power. Three of them—Jake, George, and Carl—would retire from the company decades later. These were steady, reliable, hardworking men, sons of the land transported by dearth of opportunity to an urban setting. Like the immigrants pouring into the northern and western cities, they were inward-looking, unsophisticated, wary of strangers, comfortable living and working among their own.

Older cities like New York and Boston typically have secure underground power lines running alongside sewer systems and subway tunnels dug when labor was cheap and the job didn't involve tearing up the town. Atlanta's lines run through the treetops, and, a full century after they were strung, the city is still subject to massive outages triggered by crashing limbs felled by wind and ice.

Jake Loudermilk worked a tough and dangerous job. His crew didn't have augurs to bore into the clay; they had to dig post holes by hand with specially shaped shovels, then haul the massive poles up, secure them, and string the wires. When he was on the job, there wasn't much in the way of switches, fuses, and safety equipment; the danger of electrocution was very real. Yet, thanks to his diligence, no one in his crew was ever killed or seriously injured. This was a source of pride to him and his men. Jake took care of his people. He knew his business.

While many affluent families didn't have a telephone, we did. In fact, we had a phone before we had an indoor toilet. Phones were so new, in fact, that they used only four numbers. All Georgia Power managers

Opposite: Jake's parents were William Henry and Buela Lee Ayers Loudermilk. The Loudermilk family back row: Carl, George, and Jake upper right. Front from left to right: Randolph, Mary, and Clara, with William Henry directly behind her. Buela Lee is lower right with Lucybelle seated behind her.

had phones installed so they could contact linemen in the event of power outages, which, given Atlanta's unpredictable and often violent weather, were commonplace. The calls always seemed to come between 2:00 and 6:00 A.M. Jake would stagger out of bed, pull on his boots and work clothes, and then head downtown to the power company's headquarters at 211 Decatur Street, near Five Points. When the outages were bad, he and the other workers would pile into their trucks, work twelve-hour shifts, sleep on cots, and then start all over again the next morning. Sometimes, he'd be gone for weeks at a time. Except for these emergency sessions when you could rake up the overtime, Jake was a salary man through and through. Punch in, work forty hours, punch out, and go home.

He rarely shared stories with us, but one stands out in my memory because I think it says a lot about his world and our city. During one of these emergency out-

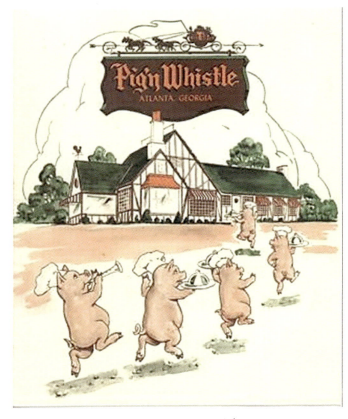

Exhausted from responding to an overnight emergency power outtage, Charlie's father Jake was refused service at the Pig'n Whistle restaurant due to his dirty work attire.

ages, my father and his exhausted crew walked into the Pig'n Whistle, a popular restaurant on Ponce de Leon Avenue. They were promptly refused service because they were grimy and dressed in work clothes. Given Jake's insecurity about his background and education, it really tore him up. Word went out quickly among all the Georgia Power crews: when the power on that particular stretch of Ponce de Leon went down, the Pig'n Whistle and its oversized neon sign depicting a pink pig playing a horn would always be last on the list of repairs.

My father, like so many blue-collar workers, was essentially mute at a time when the written and spoken word was the voice of commerce, social advancement, and cultural exchange. Jake was an outsider, albeit a stubborn one, distrustful of individuals and institutions—the world itself—he didn't understand. He never went to a movie. Wouldn't have anything to do with our schooling. Never asked about grades or homework despite the fact Mother was president of the PTA. When I finished college, my goal was to become a millionaire. I never slacked off chasing that dream. Many years later, there was an article in the Atlanta paper proclaiming me a millionaire. My father would never acknowledge that he'd seen it or knew anything about the story. My success would have been as incomprehensible to him as if I'd gone to the moon.

And yet, he was generous and good-hearted enough to cosign a loan for one of his crew. Of course, he didn't realize that when the guy defaulted, he was on the hook and had to make good out of his own pocket. Years later, when I'd run into these old Georgia Power linemen, I'd ask them, "Did you ever know my dad?"

"You mean Jake!" they'd exclaim. "Oh yeah! Great guy!"

I'd stand there gaping, and they'd say, "I know about you, Charlie. You and your mom, y'all got a restaurant." That's the first time I realized he was acknowledging me and wasn't saying negative things.

His great fear was finding himself old and broke—his father's fate. Given the times, he was distrustful of banks. He carried $100 bills around in his wallet, three, four, or five of them, a hell of a lot of money. They were his security blanket. Mother was not immune to such fears either. Until the day she died, she kept asking me, "Charlie, are you going broke?" My father didn't know or care about investments, but he put away money every payday. He'd buy U.S. Savings Bonds or Liberty Bonds—$17.50 for an instrument that paid $25 ten years later. He'd hide them in the house. I never knew where. When he passed, we opened his safe deposit box. There was a bunch of them in there that were twenty or thirty years old.

When he was young, Jake couldn't afford a car. Later on, he decided he'd buy himself a Chevrolet station wagon, a white one. The big day came. Still dressed in his boots and work clothes, he walked into Central Chevrolet on Peachtree Street. In those days, the sticker on the window would read $4,000, but you could buy it for $3,000. You had to make an offer. Haggling was unseemly to Jake. He'd rather pay the sticker price. In any event, the Buckhead salesmen took a look at him and decided he wasn't worth their time. They wouldn't even acknowledge he was in the showroom. That's the kind of invisibility black people suffered all the time. Hell, he had the cash right there in his pocket.

Jake liked routines; it's a trait I've inherited. He got paid every two weeks. The moment he stepped off the streetcar on Howell Mill Road that night, he'd walk into Bill Springer's store, cash his paycheck, and settle Mother's grocery bill. It might run $10 or $12. It was a time, long-since lost, where you'd establish credit, not with credit cards or FICO scores but with your good name and reputation.

The two men had a ritual: when the tab was settled, Bill would reach into a jar of loose penny candy and fill up a sack—a little of this and a little of that—and hand it to Jake as a bonus. When my father got home, Jim and I would be waiting. We knew when payday was. He'd hand the sack of penny candy to us. Man, it was a big deal. I think it made him proud to do it.

He remained very much a simple country fellow his whole life. He kept a garden on our fifty-by-one-hundred-foot lot. He raised a pig on it every year. During the first cold snap after Thanksgiving, we slaughtered the pig. We'd kill and dress that hog, string it up by its hind legs, gut it and all that. No one had an electric refrigerator then, so you had to do something with the meat quickly.

One autumn, my father ordered me to shoot the hog. Pigs are intelligent animals. I knew that hog, and he knew me, but I had to take a .22 rifle and shoot him between the eyes. Bang! He collapsed like someone had pulled a carpet out from under him. My father saw this as a rite of passage. I guess it was. For the rest of my life, I never hunted anything but birds.

There were other rites of passage, too. My brother Jim and my cousin Vernon Yates, (my father's sister's son), were four years older than I was. They were pretty good friends. One time, my father let them fight it out in the backyard to see who was the "best." It was a hell of a fight, but 99 percent of parents would have broken it up.

Jake didn't drink and wasn't violent, which was unusual at a time when corporal punishment was commonplace and accepted. I only recall him whipping me one time when I was eight or nine. It was on a Saturday morning, and for whatever reason, he'd ordered me to stay in the yard. Just one of those things fathers do. You don't ask, "Why?" I ignored him and went next door to play with the neighbor boy. We were smoking "rabbit tobacco," a weed rolled up in a piece of paper. I remember that because I had a bunch of wooden matches in the back pocket of my overalls.

"Charlie! Get over here!"

My father grabbed me, picked up a board, and starting beating my behind. He hit me so hard the matches ignited and smoke began pouring out of my overalls. Next thing I know, my mother's on the back porch hollering, "Stop it! Stop it! You're killing him!"

It's funny now, but it wasn't funny then.

In my father's world, everything was black or white, right or wrong. There were no in-betweens. He rarely showed any emotion, and he definitely didn't believe in hugging. If somebody came around the house, he'd welcome them but would not get up and shake hands. That was the hardscrabble way he was raised. In the mountains, you can't hug anybody, and you rarely shake hands.

Many years later, when my business was doing well, our family took a great deal of delight wrapping and exchanging Christmas presents. Mother was inundated with gifts, but "Jakus," as the kids called him, certainly had his share. On one occasion, my daughter Lisa found herself in his closet. She looked up and above her, on a shelf, were all Jake's old Christmas gifts, still in their wrapping paper! Untouched. Lisa believes he was absolutely incapable of expressing feelings, even those of joy or gratitude. I guess he hid his feelings in the closet.

When I turned nine or ten, he never put his arm around me or touched me again. I knew the way he was and always tried hard to please him. Until his death at age seventy-five, he never once said, "Charlie you did a great job there!"

Jake was a very good baseball player. His double second cousin (families intermarry up in the mountains) was the Hall of Fame first baseman Johnny Mize, who, over his career, played for the Cardinals, the Giants, and the Yankees. Johnny's mother was a Loudermilk. Dad played first base and outfield on Georgia Power squads that went up against Atlantic Steel, Atlanta Gas Light, and other company teams. He was the lead-off batter and could really stroke the ball. He wanted my brother and me to be good ballplayers.

Of course, I rushed to follow in his footsteps. Sort of. We'd play sandlot baseball behind the schoolhouse on Howell Mill Road. In those days, you'd start out with one baseball in the springtime. Never knew where it came from. When we'd knocked the cover off it, Dad would bring electrical tape home from work, and we'd wrap the ball in black tape. After that, you couldn't hit it too far because it kept getting heavier and heavier.

After practice, we'd run over to a little store that sold RC colas, beer, and peanuts. A cola cost a nickel. A bag of peanuts another five cents. I remember walking into that store with my friends one day, not a penny in my pocket. I decided to run up the hill to White Street and ask my mother for a nickel for a soda, which was comparable to asking for a dollar today.

"Charlie," she said, "I don't have a nickel to spare. Drink some cold water, and you'll be all right." I decided I'd never be broke again. I was maybe nine years old.

One day, I made it into the newspaper. There I was, "Jeep" Loudermilk swinging at a baseball! Man, was I proud! When my dad saw the picture, the only thing he noticed was that my stance was off. I was up on my toes.

"Charlie," he said, "you need to keep both feet on the ground. You lose power when you lift your foot." It was good advice. He just missed the bigger point.

I've asked myself "Why was I trying so hard to please a man who never responded?" I've come to believe the real challenge is understanding that I, like so many other men and women, am the product of both darkness and light, a mother whose love streamed over me like sunlight and a father as cold and distant as the far side of the moon. My life was shaped by these circumstances, but not necessarily for the worse.

CHAPTER SIX

*"If kids had problems, they'd come to see Miz' Loudermilk.
She was the momma figure at the whole camp."*

—THE FRITZ ORR CAMP

When I look back over my life for the one experience that impacted me more than any, it is far and away the Fritz Orr Camp. That a scruffy, ten-year-old street urchin nicknamed "Jeep" wound up spending eight summers rubbing elbows with the offspring of the wealthiest and most socially prominent families in Georgia seems an almost inconceivable turn of events. That a mentor like Fritz Orr would appear at the precise moment my father's influence was waning seems miraculous, but it happened. Once again, the guiding hand in this turn of events was Addie Loudermilk.

At the time, Fritz was a kind of Pied Piper roaming the streets of Buckhead in a station wagon collecting children along Peachtree Battle, East Andrews, West Paces Ferry, and other upscale streets for an after-school camp he ran in the backyard of a Habersham Road estate belonging to Charles B. Shelton. Charles had four sons who, shall we say, needed Fritz's direction. One of those boys, Thomas C. Shelton, is one of my best friends today. Charles Shelton had been a classmate of Franklin Delano Roosevelt's at Yale. When the president passed through Atlanta en route to the Little White House in Warm Springs, he'd often spend the night at Shelton's home.

Fritz, long deceased, still has a magical reputation among certain generations of Buckhead boys and girls. He wasn't rich, but he'd married well. His credentials were impeccable—a University of Georgia alum and a splendid horseman. Fritz was gracious and charming. He wasn't a businessman, but he was a good man who wanted the best for his charges, many of whom were lonely or unhappy despite their parental wealth. Fritz had the greatest personality of anyone I've ever known. Mothers adored him; kids were drawn to him like a magnet. As I said, a Pied Piper.

Opposite: Fritz and Augusta Orr treating the kids to a fun-filled, old-fashioned stagecoach ride at camp.

In those days, it was not unusual for people of means to travel abroad for eight or ten weeks during the summer. Their children, for the most part, were left to the nannies, butlers, and chauffeurs. When Fritz decided to expand his after-school operation into a summer camp, it seemed a natural thing for a select group of parents—many tied to the Trust Company of Georgia—to finance an available parcel of land bordering West Paces Ferry Road, West Wesley Road, and Nancy Creek Road. These investors were issued non-interest-bearing bonds, and the plan was for Fritz to pay off the bondholders over time out of camp revenue. Better yet, the parents would have a secure, guilt-free haven at which to deposit their kids.

By the time the camp really got going, Fritz was attracting campers from as far away as Augusta, Athens, and Savannah. The families of the Coca-Cola Bottlers—that's where the real money was back then—lined up to send their children to his camp. Fritz oversaw about two hundred boys and girls—less than half were overnight campers—and fifty counselors and staff. The day campers were picked up at their houses at 8:00 A.M. and returned around 5:00 P.M. The program ran a full eight weeks, which was a long time for the full-time campers to be separated from their mommies and daddies.

One of Fritz's biggest challenge was feeding all these hungry boys and girls on what was likely a shoestring budget. Fritz approached Jessie Abercrombie, the woman who oversaw Atlanta's public school cafeterias, looking for a recommendation for a dining room manager.

"Addie Loudermilk is the best we have," Abercrombie replied. "But I don't know whether she can do it. She has a family."

Sure enough, Fritz appeared at the door of our house on White Street to interview her. Then in her early forties, Mother was already two steps ahead of him.

"I'd like the job, and I need the job," she said, "but I've got this ten-year-old roaming the streets all day [this was no exaggeration], and I can't just leave him."

"Well, bring him with you!" Fritz boomed.

I imagine my mother smiling at such an ingenious solution. Me? I was both curious and nervous about venturing into this strange new world.

Neither of us realized it at the time, but Mother had done more than win me a slot in a ritzy summer camp. She had brought me in contact with a man who would become a surrogate father. Given opportunity, I blossomed under Fritz's careful eye. I forged strong links in a chain of friendships and connections I've maintained my entire life. I learned sportsmanship, horsemanship, and discovered my "people skills" extended beyond the street corner. I was a hell of a boxer and became an instructor and then a counselor. The heavy burden of insecurity that hung over me whenever I'd ventured beyond Howell Mill Road began to lift on the horseback riding trails and athletic fields that crisscrossed what is now the Westminster School.

Mother quickly put her stamp on the operation. She believed that healthy children needed lots and lots of fresh vegetables. And in her own inimitable way, she made that happen. Twice a week, she'd get up at 5:00 A.M. and drive one of Fritz's beat-up station wagons (somehow she'd learned to operate an automobile) to the farmers' market on Lee Street in the West End. She'd poke the lettuce, squeeze the tomatoes, bargain those shrewd farmers down to the last penny, and load up the back of that wagon. She could have easily ordered produce from a local wholesaler, from this, that or the other outlet. She insisted, "her boys would have the freshest vegetables."

Then she'd drive back north to the end of the streetcar line on Howell Mill and Collier Roads, pick up Moselle and two other cooks, and prepare a hearty breakfast for the full-time campers and staff members. They'd clean up, move on to lunch, and then supper. For all that, Mother earned $25 a week, less 25 cents a day for my meals.

Soon, every camper was one of her "boys." Many of the kids, both boys and girls, would come to see "Miz Addie" when they were feeling homesick or ill. Over the ten years she worked there, many lonely kids would lean on Addie's shoulder. She always found time to mother them and doctor them and listen to them. Despite my pestering, she kept all their secrets. For some children, my mother or some chauffeur or maid were the only comfort they had. No one ever asked her to do this. It was her nature to help. She loved boys. She had two of her own.

I'm also sure some campers looked at Mother as simply hired help. Maybe she was. Fritz certainly appreciated her as a worker and for everything she did to make his camp successful, but appreciation didn't get you far in Buckhead. Mother was never invited to any of the parties that Fritz and his wife hosted at their home on the hill above the camp. Neither was I.

In the afternoons, Mother usually had a few hours down time between lunch and supper. She'd walk over to where the activities were in full swing. I'd be swimming in the pool, maybe boxing or riding one of the camp horses, and sometimes I'd catch her out of the corner of my eye, beaming at me.

At the end of the day when Moses, the dishwasher, finished his chores, she'd walk down to the station wagon, legs aching from standing on her feet all day, drive her workers back to the streetcar stop, and then head home alone. She'd do it all over again the next morning. She never complained, made excuses, or tried to explain what drove her. I can imagine my father, feeling his authority slipping away, muddling over a newspaper, ignoring her when she walked in to grab a few hours' sleep. Or worse, he'd grump she'd never be the mother that his mother was.

This was her life. I was her life.

⟶⟐⟵

I remember Fritz being quoted in a magazine article. Over the years, the camp's excellent reputation made him something of an expert on youth counseling.

"The disadvantaged kids are the wealthy kids," he insisted. (I'm quoting from memory here.)

The 1947 Fritz Orr Camp staff. Charlie is in the second row, second in from the left.

"They're the ones who can't go out in the yard and play, or kick a ball around with their friends. Growing up poor gives you the big picture in life. It builds you."

Today, I feel sorry for some of the wealthy kids who never had to work. At the time I felt different and apart. They all went to E. Rivers on leafy Peachtree Battle Avenue, or R. L. Hope on Piedmont Road. I went to E. P. Howell at the end of White Street listening to the freight trains clang and whistle. Seaboard's Howell Yards was a repair facility for the coal-burning locomotives. Their soot blanketed our neighborhood. The rich kids had chauffeurs and maids. I had a calf and a friendly pig I wound up shooting. In the phrase of the time, I was not their "grade." Jeep was an outsider looking in on a closed and privileged world. I didn't possess their casual confidence and, at first, didn't recognize the neediness behind the masks many of these kids wore.

I spent three summers with Fritz as a camper and the next five as a junior and then a senior counselor. I was more suited to being a worker bee than a vacationer. I moved up the ranks as World War II inevitably depleted the camp's staff. Fritz quickly learned he could depend on me to get things done. (He didn't expect the rich boys to do any work.) I started driving a truck for him when I was sixteen.

The Fritz Orr Camp in 1947 with Charlie standing solo on the side of the truck.

He also put me in charge of the pool, which I handled pretty well, except for the time I dumped in so much chlorine that it turned the blond hair of the daughter of Dr. Thornton, Atlanta's best-known orthopedic surgeon, grass green. She was a real tomboy and couldn't care less. Daddy was none too pleased.

Boxing quickly became my specialty. I could whip anyone in the camp—thanks, no doubt, to my street brawling experience—and Fritz eventually made me the coach. Busting some snob in the nose seemed like wonderful therapy; it did earn me respect, but the truth is I had a sensitive side.

When I made counselor, I was responsible for the well-being of the eight young men in my cabin. I remember one time we were sitting on the sleeping porch, and boys being boys, the talk quickly turned to sex. Fritz, who was straitlaced, overheard us and came over and gave us a little lecture. I was maybe fourteen or fifteen.

"You know, the human race is the only species that can have sex without the expectancy of pregnancy and children," he said.

I hadn't thought of that, but it's the truth.

"In animals and everything else," he continued, "it's for propagation."

We all nodded with great seriousness. Satisfied, Fritz walked off. We all looked at each other. "*Who cares!*"

Some nights, I would sit up with a homesick boy. We'd rock on the swing Fritz had set up by the pool, and I'd talk to him until he was ready to sleep. Next morning, the kid would wake up, and it'd be all right because everyone was running around doing stuff.

When my turn came to leave for the service, I joined the U.S. Navy on my eighteenth birthday—July 12, 1945. I loved those kids from camp, and they loved me. They wrote me letters every day when I was undergoing basic training in Maryland.

I mentioned that Fritz Orr wasn't much of a businessman. At the end of the summer when it came time to pay me, he'd say, "What do you think you ought to have?"

"I don't know," I'd answer.

"How about $150?" Fritz asked.

"Sure."

"What are you going do with that?" he challenged.

"I want to take flying lessons!"

The next year was the same.

What do you think you ought to have? Would you be happy with $150?"

"Yes! I want to buy a Model A Ford!"

He probably didn't have to pay anything. He was so charismatic and most of us were having so much fun, we would have worked for free.

It's our nature to recall bitterness more intensely than sweetness. Like a wasp sting or a snakebite, youthful humiliation can really fester. And yes, I got my share of that with Fritz as well. I remember a day that some of the boys decided to take up a collection for the dishwasher's birthday. Moses was a tall black man with one of those terrible speech impediments that make you the butt of jokes. However, the kids instinctively saw what their parents would probably have missed. Moses was a gentle man and had a good heart. We loved Moses.

Anyway, I was standing there as they passed around the hat. One of the older boys, Roy Dorsey, casually reached into his shirt pocket, pulled out a dollar bill and threw it in. Then it was my turn. I didn't have a penny on me, and I had to stand there burning with shame as the hat passed me by. I felt everybody's eyes boring into me. I will never forget that moment.

Or the time I lost my shoes. Those first summers, I followed Fritz around like a little dog. I just adored the guy. Bursting with energy and, I guess, a desire to impress him, I jumped over a hedge. And

Charlie loved his role as riding instructor at Fritz Orr Camp.

lost my shoes. These were slippery, down-at-the-heels shoes that flipped and flopped when I walked. Fritz looked at me like he was seeing me for the first time.

"Charlie," he said, "you need to wear different shoes."

I didn't have other shoes.

Of course, Mother would have bought me a pair of shoes had I asked, but I was the only one without them, and I knew it. I had to stand there with Fritz and those other boys looking at me funny. In my neighborhood, we went around barefoot except to go to Sunday school.

I didn't know much about hygiene either. Mother was always working, and my father wouldn't have noticed. My brother Jim and I tried, though not very hard, to keep ourselves clean between our once-a-week baths. I remember being in the third or fourth grade. One of my teachers was talking about tooth decay. "When I get up, the first thing I do, is brush my teeth," she said.

"Well, this woman is crazy!" I thought. "She can't go to bed without brushing her teeth!"

Sometimes, you get the bitter *and* the sweet. One summer, an outbreak of polio forced Fritz to shut down the camp. Today, the terror that the crippling disease engendered in the days before the Salk vaccine seems unimaginable. But that summer, Fritz sent most of the campers home. Unfortunately, however, by the time he made the decision to close the camp, a dozen or so campers had parents who were out of the country and unreachable. Typically, Fritz turned a potential disaster into adventure. He loaded ten horses on a carrier and packed all of us, plus tents, sleeping bags, and camping gear, into a beat-up Model A Ford truck and headed up to North Carolina's Pisgah Mountains. Moses and Jimmy Porter, Fritz's brother-in-law, came along to help out.

The wooden-sided truck was packed with hay, oats, sleeping bags, and the food Mother had prepared for us. Its top was covered with canvas in case it rained. The canvas flapped in the wind. A kid named Jake Johnson and I rode up on top, legs dangling like Tom Sawyer and Huck Finn floating down the Mississippi. The overworked four cylinder motor overheated every few miles. On one of our stops to take on water, a "good old boy" mechanic took one look at the engine's white-hot head and marveled, "Who ever sent y'all up here in these mountains in this truck has the faith of Jesus!"

We camped by the Davidson River. We rode horses and generally had a fantastic time. For a street kid, I took naturally to the outdoors. Out hiking one day, I spotted a salamander almost invisible against the foliage. None of the other kids had seen it. I proudly pointed it out.

Out of the blue, Fritz turned to the group and said, "You can say what you want about Charlie, but he's got great eyes."

Why did he say that? Who was saying things about Charlie?

I felt like I'd been kicked in the gut. As much as Fritz cared about me—and he did—he unconsciously revealed that he saw me differently from the rest of them, which, I guess, I knew. But it reminded me that there wasn't anyone out there I could really bond to. No one in my condition. When I look back to those days, I can honestly say these kids were not unkind to me. They just weren't very kind.

Another time, I literally ran away from camp. I walked all the way home, about eight miles, because I couldn't take whatever I'd done to embarrass myself. Mother asked Fritz to go get me. He showed up at our house, and I returned, willing to give it another shot. Of course, I got over it. In fact, I realized that if I'd had money, I would have bought a camp of my own and worked with kids the rest of my life. I like people and work. Not books.

Whoever I was, and wherever I came from, Fritz saw something in me that he recognized, but, given the blinders of social class, he couldn't quite fathom. I think that what he saw was the furious determination to succeed that Mother had kindled in me. When I messed up in school Mother mentioned my grades to Fritz.

"Miz Loudermilk," he told her. "You don't have to worry about Charlie. He's going to do well."

Years later, at the University of North Carolina at Chapel Hill, I contemplated running for student body president—an extraordinary leap of faith. Fritz was the man I turned to for advice. He asked about my grades, and I told him they were not very good, but I *loved* student politics. He advised me that I was spending too much time on extracurricular activities and needed to concentrate more on my studies. I mostly took his advice.

It was Fritz I turned to when my father's crude behavior with another woman broke my heart; Fritz who sponsored me, a young entrepreneur, at the Rotary Club. It was Fritz who saw me on the threshold of success before he passed away. He was gone already when Mother passed, but the bonds we'd forged proved strong. In my grief, I glimpsed Polly, one of his daughters, in the crowd at the funeral.

Augusta and Fritz Orr at their home they called "high heaven," in Sapphire Valley, NC on the grounds of Camp Merrie Woode which they bought in 1951.

Chapter Seven

"Anybody can be a millionaire if he or she works hard enough."
—Charlie Loudermilk

In the fall of 1941, I was a sophomore at North Fulton High. I'd transferred to the elite public school—none too willingly—after a year with my neighborhood buddies at Fulton High School, a nickel's ride on the streetcar to where Turner Field stands today. My brother Jim had graduated from Fulton a year before. An exceedingly bright student, he'd struggled with the lowered expectations, absence of mentoring, and lack of opportunities that were typical of working-class schools. Jim had been shunted into "distributive education," a work/study program that had him working half-days during the week and all day on Saturday with the mechanics at Ralph Cannon Buick on Techwood Drive. I guess it says something that he went on to graduate from Georgia Tech in three years with a degree in aeronautical engineering.

At Georgia Tech, Jim was blackballed by the two most popular fraternities, Chi Phi and Sigma Alpha Epsilon (SAE), most likely because none of the fraternity brothers knew who he was. Fraternity rush committees didn't see many prospective Fulton High School grads.

"You've *got* to go to North Fulton," Jim said to me one afternoon. "It's really the best school."

Mother was standing next to him, nodding.

Many of the kids I'd met at Fritz Orr's camp attended North Fulton, as did my "rich" cousin, Lee Pinkard, who drove around in a souped-up prewar Mercury that Uncle Durrell had given him. Lee had come a long way since our Saturdays selling cokes in front of his father's dry cleaning store. He had a reckless streak and an ability to bend the truth any way that he wanted, which got worse as he grew older. He bragged to the Buckhead boys about how tough I was. He got me into a fight behind the school, and the guy thoroughly kicked my ass.

Opposite: Always looking out for him, Charlie's brother Jim insisted Charlie attend North Fulton High in order to get the best education he could. Addie agreed of course. Jim went on to get a degree in aeronautical engineering.

Lee could forge Uncle Durrell's signature perfectly and did so, writing excuses for his many absences. Back then, his father felt that Lee could do nothing wrong. Despite all the property he'd inherited and his dry cleaning business, Uncle Durrell was on the road to bankruptcy in the sixties, and he was becoming increasingly despondent. Years later, the phone call Mother and I had long dreaded finally came. We jumped into a car and drove out to Durrell's house. He'd long since lost the big house where he'd hosted so many extravagant parties. We found him sprawled on a chair in his backyard, a bullet hole in his head. I choose to remember him and Aunt Elizabeth, happy and full of life, showing up at our house loaded with Christmas presents.

To get to school, I had to catch the streetcar downtown each morning, then transfer to the north-bound line on Peachtree Road. And do it all over again in the afternoon. At Fritz Orr's camp, I'd gotten by with shorts and a swimsuit. At school, I didn't have the khakis and polo shirts that many of the other boys wore. I was also conscious of my street accent, especially when there were girls around.

All the boys joined the ROTC during the war, and I remember being called down unexpectedly to be fitted for my uniform. I didn't have any underwear on. I was the only boy without underwear. I hopped in and out of those pants like I was in a potato sack race. Funny how things stick with you.

In the long run, Mom and Jim were right: North Fulton made a huge difference in my life. The confidence I lacked in the classroom I reclaimed on the football field. Small but tough, I played both ways—running back and cornerback. High school fraternities were a big deal back then. Lee got me accepted into Sigma Phi Omega. I believe my lifelong affinity for politics took root there.

Other influences were subtle and lasting. When you struggle up, you're forced, inevitably and painfully, to leave your childhood friends behind. The gap between who you were and what you want to be is simply too great. At North Fulton, I met guys who would become lifelong friends. My high school buddy, Jim Barton, is eighty-two now, still runs his business out of an office a few floors down from mine. We go to lunch nearly every week.

It was at North Fulton that I met the redoubtable Ivan "Ike" C. Rolader, who would be my best friend for the next sixty years. We were born eight days apart, and, later, we found out that our mothers went to high school together. At school, we played football together—he was one of the "dirty, greasy linemen"—and on Saturdays, we worked the meat counter at a Big Star on Ashby Street on the south side of town. After high school, we were roommates in college and joined the U.S. Navy together. We even dated the same girl at least once that I recall.

Over the years, Ike and I would spend thousands of hours talking, trying to sort out lives and careers and relationships. Our wives would be friends. We'd take trips and vacations together. Our children, particularly my daughter Lisa, regarded our families and homes as interchangeable. We had a hell of a lot of fun. Neither of us was interested in studying, but Ike graduated from dental school at Emory University and went on to become a successful orthodontist, and here I am, staring at an honorary PhD on my wall.

Ike and Charlie—best friends for life.

In many ways, Ike was my mirror image. His family lived above a little filling station on what is now Northside Parkway—today, a bustling chicken restaurant operates on the spot—south of West Paces Ferry Road. During the war, rubber was rationed, and tires were in extremely short supply. Ike kept busy patching inner tubes and changing flats, many for workers commuting to the Marietta Bell Aircraft plant.

People forget such things, but hundreds of the B-29 Super Fortresses that turned the tide in the Pacific were built in Marietta. Later, the Roladers lived in a log cabin—today it would be considered "historic"—on a section of Moore's Mill Road we called "Red Ridge." His daddy was a hustler who leveraged the money he made delivering spring water and used it to buy up a lot of property. Visiting Ike was stepping back into the nineteenth century; the cabin was dominated by a huge hearth with wood smoke curling from a stone chimney and dishes of food and cakes covered by folded tablecloths to keep the flies off.

I came of age during the war. After the December 7, 1941, attacks on Pearl Harbor, our government did a tremendous job rallying the nation. Newspapers, radio, Hollywood movies—everywhere you looked it was "Hate the Japs.... Hate the Germans." My brother Jim was already overseas, assigned to a subchaser in the Pacific. I was still at home, planning to clear out the Japanese all by myself.

In the spring of 1943, Ike and I were sixteen-year-old seniors counting the days till our eighteenth birthdays when we would be able to enlist. You could not join the service without your parents' signature until you were eighteen. So we decide to stay an extra year at North Fulton and play football (I'd conveniently flunked an English course I needed to graduate). Coaches don't change much; our football coach quickly okayed the scheme. Then I miscalculated and announced to Mother that not only am I not graduating, but I'm holding myself back a year and enlisting in the navy.

"No, you're not!" she warned. "I've got one son with his life in the balance, and I don't want another going in until he has to go."

Soon enough she was on the phone with my high school principal.

"What's Charlie need to graduate?" she demanded.

I can imagine the man thumbing through my sad little transcript.

"One English course."

"Sign him up for summer school. He'll be there!"

And I was. After class, if no one picked me up, I'd the walk four miles down West Paces Ferry Road to Fritz Orr's camp. Mother was still running the kitchen and did so until she opened her own restaurant. West Paces was *the road* in Atlanta. I'd stare at the spectacular houses and a flood of complex feelings would swirl through me. I was envious . . . no, *envy* is not the word. What I felt was more visceral; someday, I'd be the guy sitting on the porch looking across *my* rolling, landscaped lawn.

That fall, I enrolled at Georgia Tech. My years with Fritz Orr were paying unexpected dividends. I didn't study much—going off to war was all I could think about—but I was rushed by the two best fraternities. I knew many of the members from camp. I ended up pledging Chi Phi. Suddenly, I was dating a girl whose father was president of a bank! I don't remember exactly how I lost my virginity, but I know I was trying a lot.

On July 12, 1945, my eighteenth birthday, I enlisted in the Navy. Ike Rolader, who did stay at North Fulton that extra year, was there with me. I didn't even bother taking final exams, and I was forced to leave Fritz Orr's camp in the middle of the session. The fish-out-of-water was becoming a sailor in the U.S. Navy, but I was experiencing that same mix of emotions I'd felt so often at the Fritz Orr Camp. The boys in my cabin wrote me every day even just a line or two to cheer me up.

I'd left home for the first time on a train bound for the U.S. Naval Training Center in Bainbridge, Maryland. Funny, the things you remember so many years later. After getting off the train and collecting our bags, we rode buses into the naval base. It was 7:00 P.M. on a summer night, and the guys who'd already eaten supper were hanging out the windows of the two-story barracks.

"You'll be sorry!" they hollered.

I looked up and saw all these boys, all my age, all competing for what I wanted, a berth on a warship.

Opposite: Charlie was eager to join the navy, even risking high school graduation. Addie wouldn't stand for it!

And behind them, I saw the hundreds of thousands of boys—the millions of boys—who I was going to have to compete with successfully to do anything in life. It was an awakening.

Germany surrendered in the spring of 1945, but the Pacific War was still raging. General Douglas MacArthur was planning to invade the Japanese mainland. Japanese Prime Minister Hideki Tojo and his fanatics had ordered the nation's women, schoolboys, and old men to resist the "barbarian" invaders to the death. In August, atomic bombs were dropped on Hiroshima and Nagasaki. The emperor surrendered a few days later. That nuclear attack might have saved my life because the navy was training us to hit the beaches alongside the marines.

I wound up playing football for a team the navy fielded out of Bainbridge, Maryland. I even got to scrimmage against the Naval Academy team at Annapolis. I remember one of the recruits I sat next to on the bus to Annapolis was wearing a big ring.

"What's that?" I asked.

"The Rose Bowl."

He'd played in the Rose Bowl.

My football career ended after ten weeks. I was homesick, and I went on leave without informing the coach. The southbound trains were jam-packed and hot; the cars filthy and littered with trash. I must have scratched my arm as I slept on the floor. And I guess the silver bracelet I wore must have rubbed and caused an abrasion because I got an infection. But I didn't pay any attention to it; all I was thinking of was surprising Mother. That morning, I got off the train at Brookwood Station, threw my duffle bag over my shoulder and walked home.

The next thing I know, my arm is discolored and swollen. This is before antibiotics, so blood-poisoning (septicemia) was even more serious then. Unchecked, a staph infection could be fatal. Mine continued to get worse.

"You've got to go to the hospital," Mother said.

I spent the next two weeks at Lawson V.A. Hospital in Chamblee, Georgia. I don't remember much beyond this gigantic flagpole out front with Old Glory waving in the breeze. When I got back to Maryland, the football coach was seriously unhappy.

"What are you doing here?" he yelled. "You're off the team!"

After basic training, Ike was assigned to Mayport, a naval base outside Jacksonville, Florida. I spent the next nine months at the Casco Bay Naval Station in Portland, Maine. As it happened, my girlfriend from Georgia Tech was working in Jacksonville, and, sure enough, she and Ike started dating while I was in Maine freezing my ass off. During the war, huge battleships berthed in Portland, and to protect them from the German U-boats prowling the East Coast, the Seabees had constructed curtains of steel antisubmarine nets at the mouth of the harbor. The subs would run into the nets setting off bells and little, wood-hulled sub chasers would go after them with depth charges. With the war over, Seaman Loudermilk's job was to drag the nets out into the ocean and dump them.

I became friendly with my second-in-command, a lieutenant j.g. (junior grade). He and I both had girlfriends at a nearby women's college. When I told him that I'd planned to go back to college that fall, he was decent enough to arrange for a speedy discharge. By some odd coincidence, I was discharged in Boston on my birthday, July 12, 1946, exactly a year to the day after I'd enlisted. If I had gotten out even a day earlier, I would have been called up for the Korean War. I wasn't. But my brother Jim, who'd joined the reserves, was.

Ike got out at the same time I did. We had a high school classmate, Bill Crosswell, whose father had attended the University of North Carolina at Chapel Hill and the two of them enrolled up there. Our brief time in the service had changed us, expanding our horizons beyond the "them vs. us" insecurities of high school. We'd met people from all over the country who didn't know Buckhead from a hole in the ground and couldn't care less what side of the tracks I had come from. America was becoming a meritocracy, which to me is one of the keys of our country's greatness.

I hoped to follow Ike to Chapel Hill, but that disastrous academic year at Georgia Tech hung around my neck like an anvil. When I look back, I believe I could have made all A's at school if I'd tried, but my focus—my gift—was on people skills. It still is.

Today, the vital quality I look for in a manager is the ability to communicate. I'm not talking rah-rah salesmanship or self-promotion; that's significant, but empathy is more important. That means taking the time to put yourself in another person's shoes whether that person is a colleague, customer, or co-worker; trying to listen and understand his or her needs, hopes, and desires; and, above all, being fair and honest.

One of the board members of the Fritz Orr Camp was Judge Luther Z. Rosser, Chi Phi's national director who kept an office in the Connally Building in downtown Atlanta. Bald and imposing, Judge Rosser had a distinguished career as a trial lawyer before being elevated to the bench. He was lead defense attorney in the controversial Leo Frank case that rocked Atlanta in 1913.

In any event, I'd been initiated into Chi Phi at Georgia Tech and wasted no time seeing Judge Rosser. I got to spend maybe five minutes with him, after which he ordered his secretary to write a letter saying glowing things about me to Roy Armstrong. Armstrong was the director of admissions at the University of North Carolina (UNC), also a Chi Phi.

Armstrong wrote me back: "Get good grades, and you're in."

So I enrolled at Georgia State for a quarter; took psychology, chemistry, and some other course; and made all A's. I was admitted to UNC in spring semester 1947 and spent the next three-and-a half years with Ike in Chapel Hill. For a while, five guys lived in one room in the fraternity house. Those years opened up a whole world for me. Sure, I was another nobody going to school on the GI bill, trying to

Charlie and Ike cruising in the "Red Devil."

survive on $52 a month, but, if you're interested in politics—and I was— unknown is not a bad place to start.

Most students were from Raleigh, Durham, Charlotte, and other North Carolina towns and cities. The world was a much smaller place then, and many of the other kids had already made enemies or had reputations that preceded them. I had no baggage. Most students also went home every weekend. Atlanta was too far for that, so I was always on campus, meeting new people and having fun. Always politicking. I had an uncanny ability to remember a person's name; I'd meet somebody briefly on campus and then see him a couple of months later and remember his name.

"Hello, Joe!" I'd shout.

It's fair to say Jeep became a big man on campus, a "BMOC." I was elected president of Chi Phi's Alpha-Alpha chapter, and then chairman of the Interfraternity Council . . . chairman of the University Party . . . chairman of the Student Council . . . member of the Men's Honor Council, the Graham Memorial Board, and the Drinking Society of 1799. I recall these long-ago events not so much out of ego or pride but as evidence of the wondrous possibilities of life in America. For me, success built seemingly upon success, but it was always supported on a foundation of hard work and a willingness to take a risk and live with the consequences should things not work out.

One summer, Ike and I designed what might have been the first automatic chicken feeder. He had a cousin named Cofield, a metal fabricator, who built the contraption we designed. You'd put a two- or three-day supply of feed into a top loader and let gravity take its course. Sound goofy? Well, variations on the machine are still used in north Georgia today.

Ike and I hitchhiked home to Atlanta every five weeks or so. On one of these trips, we stopped in Monroe, Georgia, to visit his girlfriend, Miff Martin, who was the only child of a local dentist. Miff's father got Ike interested in dentistry. Over dinner, I mentioned my dream of becoming a millionaire, which seemed as unreachable as it did when I was a boy.

Doctor Martin looked at me and said, "You know, you don't have to be super smart to be a millionaire. Anybody can be a millionaire if he works hard enough." I can still picture the scene around that table. I remember exactly where I was sitting. And I knew that I would work hard enough. That was the life lesson I took away from that chance meeting and the same message I pass on today: "Whatever you dream, you can achieve."

Charlie and Ike, friends, inventors, adventurers in life.

CHAPTER EIGHT

*"Well, what was I going to do?
If I'd said I wasn't going to stay, I'd be fired. If I'd said I was going to stay, I'd be telling a lie."*

—CHARLIE LOUDERMILK
CAUGHT IN A CORPORATE SQUEEZE

While I was testing my wings at college, my mother was slaving away in Atlanta. While I was partying—which I did big time—I didn't hesitate to write to her for money. Mattie, the same maid who took it upon herself to purchase underwear for Mother when she was too busy working, was careful to hide my letters from my father.

Whatever spending money I made working in the post office during Christmas break didn't last very long. Never once did Mother say, "Charlie, I don't have it," or "Charlie, you're spending too much." She happily sent it to me. When I look back at what she was sacrificing and what her own small dreams were, it's unbelievable how blind I was.

My years at UNC were not all sweetness and light. Given the exalted offices I held, I missed quite a few classes. As well, I probably held the record for most consecutive date nights, and a couple of times I got so drunk that I had to be taken to the hospital. By the spring of 1950, my senior year, the formidable Dudley DeWitt Carroll, dean of the school of business administration, had had enough of my antics. He warned me that if I missed my 8:00 A.M. class one more time I'd be suspended.

After Easter break, my friends and I would spend most weekends at the beach and return to campus late Sunday. One Sunday, I decided I wasn't going back until Monday morning because I'd injured my big toe. I convinced myself this was a legitimate excuse.

Dean Carroll didn't buy it. He told me the only way I could avoid suspension was a doctor's note excusing my absence. At the infirmary, the doctor examined my toe and listened to my description of my excruciating pain. I knew the doctor; he was a young guy who'd occasionally come by the frat house. He

Opposite: Charlie and Ike escaped to the beach for Easter break, setting the stage for a run-in with the Dean.

58

advised me that there was no way the dean would suspend me, but he also said there was no way he could write a note excusing my absence. I headed back to Dean Carroll's office.

"Well, then you're out!" the dean said.

"I'm never coming back!" I shouted. Then, reconsidering, I added, "I'm coming back in ten years after I make my mark in the business world to compare my net worth with yours!" All these years later, I still regret having said that.

In short order, I found myself standing on the side of the road with my suitcase, trying to thumb a ride to Atlanta. Spike Saunders, who ran the alumni association, happened to pass by. He pulled over and asked me what I was doing.

"The dean kicked me out, and I'm not going back!"

"I don't believe it."

I told him about missing that class. He shrugged and drove off.

Dean Dudley DeWitt Carroll—
a force not to be reckoned with.

Later, Saunders sent me a letter suggesting that it was an uncomfortable turn of events for a campus role model to be kicked out of school.

"You've got to come back," he wrote. "Too many people are wondering about you."

I returned, hat-in-hand, and buckled down in summer school and the fall semester. I carried five of the toughest business courses and graduated in December 1950. After graduation, something clicked inside my head. I swore off partying. No more drinking, I told myself, except for an occasional beer. I didn't even date. I guess, as the Bible puts it in 1 Corinthians 13:11, "...*when I became an adult, I set aside childish ways.*" It was time to make my mark. Today, in one of life's great ironies, both Dean Carroll and I have buildings named in our honor on the University of North Carolina campus.

Spike Saunders convinced Charlie to return to UNC and graduate.

My first job after college was working as a salesman for the PET Milk Company. I lived in Savannah and called on small grocers and grocery wholesalers in southeast Georgia. I did fine, although I used to joke that it was hard to sell milk in a place where "everybody has a cow."

I'd go round to the groceries, picking up damaged cans, tacking up signs, and hustling orders. In those days, it cost a grocer 13.5 cents for a can of evaporated milk. I tried to convince them that it made sense to advertise 2 for 25 cents "Specials" on Pet Milk every now and then. The concept of a "loss leader" that would draw customers to other products wasn't well known. Still, I talked them into losing money, which was kind of hard to do.

PET Milk had plans for me. They told me that since I had a college education, I could call on doctors—general practitioners since there were no pediatricians per se back then—and convince them to use PET instead of Carnation or Borden's Silver Cow condensed milk. Back then, no special formulas like Similac existed for babies. To prepare me, they sent me to school at their home office in St. Louis. What I remember most about the experience was that it was the first time I'd ever seen steak tartare.

"*What the hell? Are these Yankees eating raw meat?*"

Management advised me that they'd "spend the money to put you through school only if you promise that you're going to stay with the company."

Well, what was I going to do?

If I'd said I wasn't going to stay, I'd be fired. If I'd said I was going to stay, I'd be telling a lie. I didn't know what I was going to do, but I knew I wouldn't be staying with PET Milk. I learned a lesson up there: Don't put somebody on the spot like that and force them to lie.

Back in Savannah, I started calling on doctors. About that time, Billy Carver, my roommate suggested I apply for a position with Charles Pfizer & Co., his employer. During World War II, the chemical and pharmaceutical conglomerate had pioneered the mass production of penicillin. In 1950, it launched the antibiotic, Terramycin. Sales would top $45 million after just two years on the market.

That was all well and good. My problem was that I had no chemistry or science background whatsoever, and most of the salesmen Pfizer recruited seemed to be pharmacy or medical school dropouts. On the other hand, Pfizer was in a hurry to ramp up a sales team, and I could sell like the dickens.

I got hold of the company's little green handbook, *Terramycin*, and sat on the my porch swing for hours trying to read the damn thing. I didn't know what the hell I was reading. Not one word. However, Billy's recommendation carried enough weight to get me hired as a trainee. I headed up to Greensboro, North Carolina, to learn the pharmaceutical sales business.

I began with a two-week blitz in North Carolina with about ten other salesmen. After the blitz, I was assigned to the territory around Greensboro. I'd arrive in a town with a bunch of leads—maybe a card for every doctor, hospital, or medical building in the area. Since I had to learn the jargon and so forth, an older, experienced salesman was assigned to teach me to be a medical "detail man."

Our first call was in Highpoint, North Carolina, a bustling furniture town about fifteen miles from Greensboro. The detail man is the knowledgeable one. He pitches the doctors and cites the research and specific benefits, sometimes using testimonials from other physicians who regularly prescribe the medications. (Some of these were dubious. There was a doctor at the Medical College of Georgia who would praise anything for a price, and his reputation preceded him.) We pulled up to an old house. There were doctors' offices on both sides of a long hall. I got out of the car, lugging my satchel of samples. I expected the older man to get out of the other side. But he just sat there.

"I don't believe in two people calling on a doctor," he said. "You go by yourself."

I was scared to death. "I don't know what the hell I'm doing," I thought. "I've got to quit."

I steeled myself, went in, and asked to see one of the doctors. Around this time, Pfizer had developed a penicillin that was milled so fine that it could pass through a tiny 21-gauge needle. Until this development, pediatricians had been forced to inject babies with antibiotics suspended in sesame oil or other media using much thicker (and more painful) needles.

I thought quickly about how to make this point to my client. In those days, everyone carried fine-tipped fountain pens. You'd write and blot. Anyway, I took a syringe, aspirated the penicillin out of the bottle, and then, as the doctor looked on, proceeded to write his name in penicillin on a blotter. It puffed up, clearly visible.

"Very impressive!" he said.

He sent me over to a drugstore with the unlikely name, "Mann's Number Two."

"Tell 'Pee-Wee,' the head druggist, to put this product in for me," the doctor told me.

"Pee-Wee" was behind the counter. Yes, he was short.

"Get out of here, boy!" Pee-Wee shouted at me. "Every detail man that comes in here says the doctor wants his product put in!"

"Sir," I pleaded, "he really does want this in. It's a new product."

I stood there, staring at him. Finally, I said, "Would you at least call over across the street and talk to his secretary?"

Pee-Wee called the doctor, and my order was approved.

In another of those odd and unexpected circumstances in my life, all of a sudden, practically every doctor started prescribing Pfizer products. The blue-and-white packages were everywhere. A year later, Sam Brock, my district manager from Atlanta, came up to work with me. I took him to visit Pee-Wee's pharmacy. By then, let's say I had my sea legs. I'd literally walk in the back and help fill the prescriptions. (It doesn't take a lot of brains to put twenty-four tablets into a bottle.) The pharmacist types up the label, and it's gone.

Sam Brock wrote in the Pfizer newsletter that Mann's Number Two had more Pfizer products on its shelves than many wholesalers. The word got around fast. I was becoming a success!

In Greensboro, there was a three-story medical arts building near where I lived. Among the practitioners were a doctor and his son who shared a joint practice. Next door was the pharmacy. I went in to see the son, who was probably thirty-five or forty years old. When you're "detailing," you take something out of your bag and tell the doctor about it. When you're done, provided the doctor is still interested, you take something else out and put it on the edge of his desk and talk about that.

Pfizer was producing other important drugs, and among them was Streptomycin. This powerful antibiotic is effective against drug-resistant bacteria like streptococci and staphylococci and was also the drug of choice in tuberculosis treatment.

Anyway, this doctor sat there and let me put a sample of everything in my bag on his desk. I was talking away, hoping for a kind word. Suddenly, with his hand, he sweeps everything into the damn trash can! I was stunned.

"Doctor," I finally stammered, "I'm sorry you don't like our products. I think they're very fine."

I scooped up my samples, put them back in my bag, and walked out. I'm fighting to control my temper with this guy. I didn't realize he was a joker. About a week later, I walked into the pharmacy next door to the medical arts building.

"Charlie, I don't know what you did," the druggist said, "but everything Dr. Ravenell and his father prescribe is now Pfizer!"

Another life lesson: If I'd blown up at the man, it would have been all over. A few seconds' gratification versus hundreds of dollars in potential sales out the window. Two years later, I was Pfizer's number-one salesman. I'm working pretty much nonstop these years—no social life, no anything. The only free time I had was on Wednesdays, when for some reason, doctors typically took the afternoon off. Sometimes, I'd play golf with the detail man who sold Aureomycin, a competing antibiotic. Sometimes at night, I would hit balls by myself at the driving range.

Pfizer is big on incentives. Perform well and you'd be awarded a fishing rod, a camera, stuff like that. I collected those prizes like trophies. In due time, I was promoted to district manager in Richmond, Virginia. By then, I was the leading detail man out of Pfizer's three-hundred-man sales force. I eased up a bit when I was on top. I began to understand the importance of maintaining a balance between work and play, though, when you're young, "balance" is hard to define. I resumed carousing. Unfortunately, moving up the career ladder left me neither happy nor fulfilled. A day came when I realized that even if I had Sam Brock's job I wouldn't be happy.

I have one overriding personality trait: I'm determined to control most everything around my life. I won't allow anybody or anything to hold me back. Without control, I feel suffocated—and this goes all the way back to when I was a boy and my brother and my cousin Vernon trapped me under the house. Then, the plumber had come to my rescue. After three years at Pfizer, things were getting claustrophobic. And there were no plumbers to pull me out.

At the time, Hawaii was a U.S. territory, but it was headed for statehood. Pfizer was moving aggressively to open this new market. As top salesman, I was recommended for the job all the way up to John E. McKeen, president of the company, which was then headquartered in Brooklyn, New York. If I were Catholic this would the equivalent to meeting the Pope. I met with McKeen who lost little time passing over me.

"Too young, and he's single," McKeen ruled.

I was outraged. "I can't get any older quickly," I told Sam Brock. "And I'm not getting married to go to Hawaii!"

To be held back for no good reason really stuck in my craw. After clearing so many hurdles, my age had tripped me up? What other obstacles would arise and how regularly? I went round and round trying to figure out what to do. Today, I feel Mr. McKeen was probably right. I did have some maturing to do. Still, walking away from a successful career is a risky decision, but I was moving inevitably toward a life-altering realization: I had to be my own boss.

CHAPTER NINE

"The best food in Atlanta, and I should know."
—THE VARSITY'S FRANK GORDY ON
ADDIE'S ROSE BOWL RESTAURANT

In Atlanta, my mother had arrived at that same crossroads. Now in her mid-forties, she was an experienced food service manager, having run kitchens for "Tubby" Davis at Davis Brothers, the Atlanta Paper Company's cafeteria, "The Townhouse," a restaurant near the downtown public library, two school cafeterias, and the Fritz Orr Camp. More recently, she and a coworker named Mary McKinsey were managing the bustling lunch operation at Davison's department store (later Macy's) at 180 Peachtree Street, competing with Rich's famous Magnolia Room. Both women were skilled at preparing fresh, tasty Southern food at a time when most affordable restaurants in Atlanta were slinging hash and grease.

In 1945, McKinsey opened Mary Mac's Tea Room. A "tea room" signified food and service a few cuts above the greasy spoons scattered along Ponce de Leon Avenue. For better or worse—and I think better—fast food had not yet arrived on the American scene. Tea rooms were smaller and cozier than the big cafeterias that churned out nondescript meals the way Ford and General Motors mass-produced cars. Women owned tea rooms, a rare thing in post-war Atlanta. They brought a semblance of familiarity and family feeling to harried diners rushing to grab a decent meal in the course of a short lunch break. This was the key to success. In fact, Mary Mac's is still going strong more than sixty years later, although the ownership has changed.

That same year, my mother opened her own tea room on 17th Street between Peachtree and West Peachtree. A previous owner had christened it the Rose Bowl after Georgia Tech's first and only appearance in the post-season gala, a victory in 1929, so she kept the name. Mother could seat maybe forty-

Opposite: Charlie's parents Addie and Jake. After raising two boys, Addie
still had energy and drive to start her own restaurant, Addie's Rose Bowl.

five people and served dinner between 5:00 and 8:00 P.M. Soon enough, her Sunday lunch had the after-church crowd arriving in droves.

There was an appeal to the place that went beyond the plates piled with fried chicken, collards, mac and cheese, and country-fried steak. The food wasn't "sophisticated," but it was damn good, always fresh, and tasty. The warmth and generosity of spirit that drew so many lost boys to Mother at the Fritz Orr Camp was undiminished. Today the word would be *magnetism*. If you were alone, dragging after a long day at the office, Miz Addie would seat you among a gaggle of folks you'd never seen before. In short order, smiles were being exchanged, friendships were forming, and more than a few romances were getting underway. Bustle and clatter was my mother's natural element. You'd find her day after day, smiling and joshing with her regulars, making sure every meal was a small triumph, keeping things running smoothly among the cooks and servers, and basking in compliments she never received at home.

Her warmth radiated throughout the place, in the friendliness of the waitresses, the scuttling bus-boy, the cooks working in the steamy kitchen, the cashier sitting amidst all the tumult, the lines of hungry customers that ran up the entire block to Peachtree Street (so long that Mother eventually had to put benches on the sidewalk).

Having said all that, the Rose Bowl grossed maybe $100 on a good night. But Mother knew how to manage; she understood the need to control costs and cut down waste. She could eke out a profit serving $1.50 dinners.

When I started my company, these lessons would be more valuable than anything I had learned at college or while working as a salesman. Mother *lived* the most important lessons, working hard and honestly, treating employees fairly, giving consumers value for their hard-earned dollars. That's what drove her success, and I believe it drove mine as well.

That and luck. One Sunday, Frank Gordy, who owned the famous Varsity drive-in on North Avenue showed up after church. The Rose Bowl was jammed and, after he'd eaten, Gordy walked up and confided to the cashier, "This is the best food in Atlanta, and I should know!" The poor woman didn't have a clue who Gordy was.

Another of Mother's regulars was Mr. Folsom who owned the Pershing Point Apartments/Hotel, a landmark building then located at the point where Peachtree Street and West Peachtree intersect. (It was demolished in 1985 in one of Atlanta's regular paroxysms of development.) The building's architect was G. Lloyd Preacher, who'd also designed the Carnegie Building and the infamous Winecoff Hotel, which in 1946 was the scene of the deadliest hotel blaze in U.S. history.

Opposite: Addie found great pleasure hosting a birthday party at her Rose Bowl
restaurant for her granddaughter Lisa (center) who had just turned four years old.

At the time, Pershing Point's clientele was mostly retirees who lived in two-room apartments. All of the residents knew one another and had quite a comfortable community. Mr. Folsom decided his residents might want a place to eat on the premises.

In the mid 1950s, the nightclub, *Sans Gene*, was in the building. Its more successful counterpart, *Sans Souci*, made it, but *Sans Gene* tanked. The space could accommodate two hundred people and had been fully equipped with booths, chairs, tables, napkins, and silverware before becoming a ghost town. After watching the crowds line up night after night at the Rose Bowl, Folsom, no doubt frustrated, came by to offer Mother a deal: If she'd lease the old nightclub space and open a restaurant at Pershing Point, he'd provide the furnishings and equipment at no cost. By then, the 17th Street Rose Bowl was strangling in its own success. Mother could have served five times as many people and knew it. But she had no room to expand.

No opportunity comes without risk. The key to a successful business venture is to reduce risk, not avoid it. A restaurant is a particularly high-risk venture. Most go out of business within a few years, no matter how auspicious their beginnings. Success is rarely transferable from one restaurant to another and increased volume does not guarantee increased profits. Costs—including employee theft—often rise faster than receipts. Worse, a new space might dispel whatever *ambiance* drew people to the Rose Bowl. Still Mother was intrigued. I've always believed she was as eager to be successful as I am. Keep in mind that her sons were the most important things in her life. When Folsom made his offer, Jim was off working for Texaco, and I was a traveling salesman racking up miles and living out of a suitcase hundreds of miles from home. Mother wanted me back in Atlanta, and, yes, I missed being around her after the years in college and the military.

As a boy, the importance of *family* (whether it's conventional, convoluted, or confounding is beyond our control) had taken root in me. It remains to this day. Mother's strength—her willingness to sacrifice herself—was the heart and soul of our family. Values can be nurtured, passed on, and even strengthened over time. *Family* values—decency, loyalty, cooperation, respect, honesty, pride—are the core values that have made America the greatest country in the history of the world, and, yes, sped Aaron's success over the years.

When Mother called to tell me about Folsom's offer, I was still going round and round trying to decide what to do about Pfizer. Indecision was not what the senior management at Pfizer expected or appreciated. In those days, there was no coddling of employees. Loyalty was absolute. If headquarters discovered you were even thinking about anything but Pfizer, that was it.

I remember my boss, Sam Brock, Pfizer's vice president for southeast sales, trying to reason with me. "Charlie," he said, "you've got a great future. Why would you want to leave?" Even going that far, Brock was taking a risk. "If they knew we were even talking," he added, "*I'd* be fired." That made me think some more. It took me another week or two, and then I quit.

I returned to Atlanta welcomed by my new business partner. I'd like to say that everything was smooth as banana pudding, but neither life nor business works that way. Immediately, Mother and I ran into a challenge that would bedevil me and keep me on the brink of catastrophe for the next twenty years—securing financing to grow the business.

In simplest terms, we didn't have money to get a second restaurant up and running. As it turned out Tubby Davis, Mother's old boss, also had his eye on the *Sans Gene* space. When we applied for a loan from the Trust Company of Georgia, Tubby agreed to cosign the note. Of course, *Sans Gene*, now Rose Bowl I, was our collateral.

We kept the first restaurant—our tea room—going and threw ourselves into making Rose Bowl II a success. With two of us overseeing operations, we could stay open seven days a week, with the exception of Saturday lunch and Sunday supper. From a handful of people at Rose Bowl I, we grew to a staff of forty-five. Lunch was our biggest challenge: In those days most office workers and secretaries had just half-an-hour to eat, minus whatever minutes it took to walk to Pershing Point.

Oh, man, did we work! I move through life at great velocity, but it took everything I had to keep up. I worked the front end, greeting and seating customers, keeping an eye on the cash register like some fast-paced game show host. Mother ran the kitchen. Thirteen waitresses and two busboys scuttled round the dining room.

During lunch, we'd serve a meal every sixteen seconds. If every table was not full by 11:55 A.M., we were having a slow day. Professional cleaning services didn't exist in those days. At 8:00 P.M., when the restaurant closed, everyone had to clean his or her own station and prep for the next day's rush.

Mother was ten times more experienced than I was, but she was always willing to let me try my hand at management. I remember one time in particular. We had forty-five employees, but just one person handled the desserts and salads.

"We need two people there," I told her.

" I don't think so, but okay."

After three weeks, she asked *the question*. By the way, it's one of the keys to successfully growing a business. "Charlie," she said, "are we operating any better than we were?"

"I've got to tell you, 'No.'"

I looked around. The flow was not any better, and we were paying an extra salary. I let the new person go.

She knew beforehand what would happen, but she let me fly my wings. Over the years, I've tried to do that with Aaron's. It's not easy. Any entrepreneur looks at the enterprise as his or her own baby. In general, too many managers, from CEOs on down, have problems delegating authority and encouraging others' initiative. Either they make decisions themselves, or put off making decisions.

I moved into a one-bedroom apartment two doors from the restaurant. If my day-to-day life had shrunk to the dimensions of a tennis court, I didn't notice. I was living the dream. Soon, Mother and I poured every dollar the restaurant earned into a new business that I was starting on the side. We'd take out just enough salary to live. I took more than she did.

Life never fails to amaze me. Young Jeep, who'd scrambled up and down Howell Mill Road determined to squeeze out a hard-earned nickel here or a dollar there, is father to the man I am today. By every measure, I have lived a life, met people, saw and experienced wonders that I never could have imagined as a boy. But that Jeep is still with me—an entrepreneur surely, but a working man, too.

Eventually, Mother and I opened a third restaurant, this one in the Cox-Carlton Hotel, 683 Peachtree Street across from the Fox Theater. Like Folsom at Pershing Point, Mr. Yon, made us an offer we couldn't refuse, another fully equipped turnkey operation. In return, his guests—most seemed to be trainees attending two- or three-week insurance sales seminars held on the premises—would get great food at low prices. We decided one of our managers, Nell Missinger, could run the booming Rose Bowl II while we got Rose Bowl III up and running.

Wrong. Within six months, the Rose Bowl II had plunged into the red. Nell was way over her head as a manager, but that decision had been ours. Meanwhile, Mother and I were struggling at the Cox-Carlton, but for different reasons. No matter how hard we worked, how much we cut costs and staff, the restaurant hemorrhaged money. In short order, we'd also gone from a successful expansion to being unable to pay our bills.

The day came when Mr. Yon showed up. I was expecting the worst, but rather than shutting us down, the man taught us a lesson. "Charlie," he began, "you and your mom are killing yourselves. Something's got to be wrong here."

He knew a consulting firm, Harris Kerr Forster (today, PKF International) that specialized in restaurant management. He suggested hiring them to go over our operations with a fine-tooth comb. The fee was $1,000.00—an amount probably equal to $10,000 in today's dollars. We couldn't afford it.

"*I* want to do it," Mr. Yon insisted. "If you can pay me back, fine. If not, fine."

And that's how we discovered our profits were walking out the back door. Literally. At one point, the Harris Kerr Forster man arrived to inventory our stock of prime rib, which was transported in barrels from Chicago. An hour later, when he rechecked his count, he found the meat was missing. Same thing happened with our hams. Eventually one of Mother's long-standing employees—a woman who'd worked with her in the kitchen at Fritz Orr's—was caught sneaking out the door with a hunk of bacon hidden in her blouse.

Opposite: Addie and Charlie opened a third restaurant in the Cox-Carlton Hotel across from the Fox Theater.

Today, despite all the improvements in security, employee theft remains the ruin of many restaurants. I heard the story of a Connecticut couple who took over a TGI Friday's franchise in Canada a few years ago as part of a business settlement. They were forced to operate the business at a distance, which is a surefire recipe for disaster. Soon, they were up at all hours of the night scanning an Internet-based video camera trying to figure out which employees were looting their inventories of meat and liquor, serving free drinks and presenting understated bills to their friends. As it turned out, it was not a case of which employee; it was a matter of how many. The restaurant went bankrupt a few years later.

Mother and I were forced to build secure storerooms in the basements of Rose Bowl II and III. We hired a couple of older women to keep track of each item requisitioned by the kitchen staff. At day's end, they provided an accounting, which I ran against the receipts in the cash register. Unlike the digital video camera, it was a hands-on system, and it worked. A hell of a lesson. After years of struggles, thieves had driven us nearly to the edge of bankruptcy. But it wasn't the last time I'd be tottering on the brink of ruin.

———

I married Marilyn "Mickey" McQueen in 1956. I was twenty-nine years old. Mickey was well-bred, charming, and socially adept. In short, she was my opposite. She's the mother of my three wonderful children, Lisa, Robin, and Linda, whom I love more than life. Ironically, Mickey and I met on a double date that my buddy Tom Shelton arranged for me with Mary Ellen Jones. Mickey was Tom's date. The two girls had been friends at Washington Seminary, a private Atlanta high school for women. Mickey's father, James, was an executive with Bethlehem Steel. Mary Ellen's daddy was the golfing great, Bobby Jones. I was moving up in the world.

A year later, Mickey and I married. We had a lovely wedding at the old Saint Phillip's Episcopal Church on Peachtree Road. By far, our most expensive present was a sterling silver punch bowl, which, as you'll see, becomes the perfect metaphor for my next business career. The marriage lasted thirty-seven years. All these years later, I asked Mickey what first attracted her to me. "It was your *drive*," she said. "I'd still support you for president, but I couldn't stand being married to you—you work all the time!"

When we were courting, I couldn't afford to buy Mickey an engagement ring. It turned out that Walter R. Thomas, the well-known Atlanta jeweler, was a regular customer at the Rose Bowl. He and his secretary would show up for lunch like clockwork every day. Mr. Thomas and I made a barter arrangement. He'd sell me a diamond ring; in return, we'd run a tab against what I owed him. It took a lot of pork chops and macaroni and cheese to settle that account. In any event, Mickey traded up that engagement ring for a bigger one. I was unhappy about that. That first ring was special to me.

We'd married a little later in life than most of our peers, so we were eager to start our family. In 1957, a year after our marriage, our daughter Lisa was born; our son Robin arrived in the spring of 1959;

and Linda came five years later in 1964. As I mentioned, I'd started a business on the side, a one-man operation that rented secondhand chairs and similar supplies to auction houses and folks hosting parties. If anything, married life accelerated my work habits. I had a family to support, and that's what men do.

Not surprisingly, Mickey was not comfortable with a husband who worked twelve hours a day and seven days a week, leaving her to manage the house and look after two small babies. No young wife would have been. On her first Mother's Day morning, I got up, showered, shaved, and was halfway out the door on my way to work when she stopped me.

"Charlie," she asked, "where are you going?"

I was confused. "To the restaurant," I answered. "Mother's Day is one of our biggest days."

She cried. I am who I am.

One Christmas, I made a barter arrangement with an art dealer who ran a gallery across from the Rose Bowl III. I traded a string of lunches and dinners for a pretty good oil painting. I was proud of my negotiating skills, but I am not much of an art connoisseur. Years later, I noticed the painting had been damaged and never repaired. That really hurt.

Of course, Mother was paying for half of these presents. The money I used came out of the business, and she was my partner. A lot of partners would have said, "Hell, no!" She was delighted. Mother and Mickey grew very close, especially since Addie was determined that I spend as many weekends as I could with my wife and kids. My mother had known too much distance with my father.

In the 1960s, Ike Rolader and I shared a house at Tate Mountain, a secluded and peaceful spot on Lake Sequoyah near Jasper, Georgia. The property had been developed by "Colonel" Sam Tate who'd founded the Georgia Marble Company on land that could be traced back to the Cherokees. Sam hoped to turn the property, with its hotel and lakeside campgrounds, into a resort along the lines of Highlands, North Carolina. His family's pink marble mansion, the "Tate House," is still standing. After Sam died in 1938, the property fell into disrepair until it was bought by a group of Atlanta families who staved off a bankruptcy, formed a corporation, and sold off the lots for vacation homes. Today, Robin, Lisa, and I have our own compound up there.

I was supposed to take one weekend off and Mother was to have the next. I'd work Saturdays; she'd handle the big lunch on Sunday. But she would absolutely not hear of any such thing. Many, many weekends, she insisted I join Mickey and the kids at Tate Mountain on Friday night. I've always been one to enjoy myself. Soon enough, I had a horse and was off jumping or fox hunting, while Mother stayed in Atlanta working endless hours underwriting my lifestyle. Of course, I realize that the restaurants were her life, but it wasn't fair. I did fun things, and she paid the price.

Her love for our family flowed through our lives like a swift and pure stream. It ran so deep and vital that even my father, despite his cold nature, eventually thawed a bit, even if only in Mother's reflected warmth. My children, particularly my son Robin, grew to love my father. They called him "Jakus," a name far softer than the abrupt and unfriendly "Jake."

———— ✦ ————

Mother and I worked together for nearly fifteen years. My children's earliest memories are of Sunday lunches at the Rose Bowl. My daughter, Lisa Loudermilk deGolian, remembers filling water glasses for our customers and riding in the vintage brass elevator cages at Pershing Point. Linda is too young for those memories. I put her to work later.

My Aunt Mary, Addie's sister, returned from New York with her carpet-importer husband, Henry Surgeon. They were looking for a new career. They bought Rose Bowl III from us and rechristened the joint, "Orange Bowl," which was close enough to confuse customers. Henry, who fancied himself a bookkeeper, proceeded to run the restaurant into the ground. The restaurant business is not an easy one. Eventually, we sold Rose Bowl II as well. Mother and Aunt Mary next opened a cafeteria in Buckhead. She just wouldn't quit and worked there until her knees gave out.

I don't know where I would have wound up if I had stayed in the restaurant business. Honestly, I always saw the restaurants as a means to an end. I wanted my own company and when that happened, I wanted Mother as my partner. After all, it was her sweat and meager profits that had seeded my dream. I came of age in those restaurants. The overpowering need I had to work and hustle had matured into a lifelong passion. The competitiveness that drove me in fistfights and football games when I was younger now grew stronger. The world was growing more expansive, and I was determined to find my place in it.

As a boy, I'd tried to use dollars to define success. I wanted to be a "millionaire." But as I grew older, my dreams and hopes became more complex and difficult to define. I was living in a region of the country that would soon experience convulsive change. Atlanta as a business town was rising from the ashes of a long slumber. The Civil Rights movement was stirring. My city would become home to Martin Luther King Jr., John Lewis, and Andrew Young.

I was far-removed from all the tumult. To me, Lester Maddox and his Pickrick Restaurant was a poor competitor. But I could feel and breathe change in the air.

So many memories come flooding back as I write these words.

Part Two
Family Values

"You are our family. We'll always be there for you."

—Charlie Loudermilk
IN A MESSAGE TO ALL AARON'S EMPLOYEES

Chapter Ten

"He never sat down. She never sat down."
—Lisa Loudermilk deGolian on her father and grandmother

With the first words of this book, I set out to show how my mother's love, courage, pride, and determination put her two young sons firmly on the path to success. I've tried not only to honor her memory but also to bring her to life as the vigorous and extraordinary person she was. Along the way, I've gotten to know myself a little better.

I've been doubly blessed in that Mother's grace clearly continues to flow in her grandchildren—Lisa, Robin, and Linda—and her great grandchildren. If you'll indulge an old man's pride, I will argue again that Addie Loudermilk's family values are the core values of the company that I built and that Robin now runs.

My children were never far removed from our family's day-to-day struggles and concerns. They certainly were not born with silver spoons in their mouths, nor did they have their every whim indulged. Sometimes, I wish I'd been more affectionate and spent more quality time with them, but I've come to believe all parents are imperfect. We do the best job we can.

Lisa, Robin, and Linda are smart, strong, and willful adults, which is my way of saying that we're close-knit but don't always agree. They undoubtedly see me in ways I don't see myself. I've encouraged that. Their memories of "Granny and Jakus" are quite different from mine. Certainly, these should be included in these pages. So I'm going to step offstage for a bit and let my eldest, Lisa, share some of her memories before picking up the story again.

Addie Loudermilk was my grandmother. Today, I'm older than she was when I first called her "Granny," but my remembrances of her are as vivid and clear as a spring morning. Robin Loudermilk, president and CEO of Aaron's, and the noted fashion designer Linda Loudermilk are my brother and sister.

Opposite: Charlie and the kids make the best of a Georgia snowfall.

80

Robin is close to my age; Linda, whose acclaimed work incorporates green "eco-fabrics" is almost eight years younger. No two people, no matter how close their ties, experience the world the same way. Memory is subjective, but I've tried my best to capture as honestly as I can—albeit in fragments, impressions, and images—how Granny Addie and Charlie loved and inspired each other and, by their example, all of us.

Anyone reading this knows that "Jeep," R. Charles Loudermilk, went on to build Aaron's Inc, the most successful and innovative sales and lease ownership company in the country. He still goes to work every day and is still hurrying to "change things," pursuing personal projects as well as any number of charitable and philanthropic outreaches. Daddy is eighty-three, but thinks he's forty.

Despite the acclaim he's earned for his success and generosity, deep down, my father is a shy man. I don't think he believes he's done a whole lot. That's typical of his generation. The Greatest Generation. These are the men who came home from World War II, got an education on the G.I. Bill, worked hard, and raised their families. They never looked back; they never complained.

Today, his story stands as an inspiration to a lot of people who may think, for whatever reason, that "I'm from the wrong side of the tracks. I'll never amount to anything." Like so many of his generation, Charlie's life and career is an example of a fundamental American value: If you set your mind to something, you can do it.

Growing up in our family was never boring. When Robin and I were kids, Daddy would come home from work late every night. The realities of his life were, "We don't have any money. You get a pair of shoes for school and a pair of shoes for Sunday school. That's it. Nobody's buying anything. We're going to defrost the freezer, and we're gonna make some soup. Whatever's in there, that's what we're eating!"

And we're sitting at the table saying, "Okay, okay, we can handle this. It's going to be okay." And then a week later, he'd walk in and say, "Well, I just bought a hockey team!" And my mother would say simply, "I didn't know we needed one of those."

On the day I was born, my father was struggling to get Aaron's up and running. He was working in the Rose Bowl restaurants with Granny and had started this new rental business on a shoestring. As family legend has it, he borrowed $500 to purchase three hundred secondhand folding chairs and rented them out for a dime-a-day to auctioneers. From that modest beginning, he grew a company that this year will generate $3 billion in annual revenue, includes more than 1,600 stores in the United States and Canada, and serves millions of consumers struggling to earn their piece of the American dream.

Even as an adult, "Jeep" was caught between two worlds: the familiar world of hustle, sweat, and constant striving on one hand, and the serene, to-the-manner-born world of the post-war Atlanta community known as Buckhead on the other. Sometimes, it seemed his destiny was to relive the Fritz Orr Camp over and over again. One of my favorite stories has to do with Daddy and Ike Rolader deliver-

Lisa and her Grandmother Addie share a little girl time.

ing a truckload of Aaron's punch bowls, glasses, and party accessories for a New Year's Eve bash at the Cherokee Club on West Paces Ferry Road.

Keep in mind that these two buddies—there was hardly a spare nickel between them—had joined Cherokee "very early on" mostly to play golf, which, by the way, they seldom played. At that point in their careers, none of the other clubs in town would have accepted them. After making their delivery rounds, as Daddy tells it, he and Ike went home, put on suits ("picked up our fancy wives"), and headed back to the Cherokee Club. As the party got under way, one of the hostesses kept staring at Ike and finally walked over. He had delivered to her house that afternoon.

"Haven't I seen you recently?" she asked as Ike and Daddy cringed.

Aaron's was a part of our family. It was with us at the supper table; it was with us 24/7, on weekends and vacations; it was a fourth and often unruly sibling who demanded all of Daddy's attention. When we were five-, six-, seven-, and nine-year-olds, we knew Aaron's as well as we knew each other. At night, Dad would come from work and hurry past the typical parental questions.

"How are your grades?" or "How is this?" or "How is your friend so and so?"

"Fine," we'd answer.

"Now let's talk about Aaron's!"

His mood depended on what had happened that day. He was exhausted. He was excited. He was exhilarated. As I said, it was never boring.

"We're going into hospital equipment rental this week!"

"Also, we're going to rent Winnebagos!"

I had a wonderful childhood. For most of it, my parents didn't have a lot of money. Mother would make some of my clothes. Each week, we'd go to the Rose Bowl restaurant to pick up a big box of groceries because we could get food wholesale. On weekends, Daddy would take us to the warehouses, and we'd help wash the returned dirty dishes using big sprayers. He'd charm Ike and his other friends into helping him load the trucks, though he says they never worked as hard as they claimed. When the company went public, a number of his buddies were rewarded many, many times over.

Another favorite story. The phone rings.

"Do you rent punch bowls?"

"Absolutely!" Daddy assured the caller. "When do you need it?"

"Tomorrow."

He didn't know all our punch bowls were spoken for. He ran home and behind my mother's back, grabbed her beloved silver punch bowl, a wedding present, and snuck it out of the house. On one of these occasions, it came back with a dent that probably cost him more to fix than he'd made. Mother fretted

Lisa recalls a wonderful childhood with her mother, father, and siblings.

that he'd rent the silver flatware if she didn't keep an eye on it. He'd leverage anything. He treated Sears & Roebuck as his warehouse, purchasing whatever he needed on the fly.

I never worried growing up. I was having a good time. We children never doubted that Daddy would make it. And if he was worried, he never let us know. That's the way he is. As children, we learned there were always going to be people who had things we didn't have. Always. In the long run, we're so much the better for it.

I have friends whose fathers sat around and didn't do anything positive with their lives. Many inherited family money and never had to work. Today, they seem a little jealous of the Loudermilk kids'

Lisa, Linda, and Robin Loudermilk learned the value of hard work and resourcefulness from their father and grandmother.

"adventures." We always did stuff. Daddy is still doing stuff. He's got a factory down in Coolidge, Georgia, that manufactures furniture for the Aaron's stores. Recently, the foreman told me he saw my father pulling wood scraps out of a dumpster.

"Can't we find something useful to do with this?" my father asked.

Daddy and Granny share the same personality. They love people, and they love to work. For most people, "There's work, and then I'll go do what I want to do with my life." For them work is their pleasure. Even when our family grew comfortable, Granny continued to work hard well into her seventies when her knees began to fail. Daddy is not happy unless he has a project. He's mentioned the vacation house we shared with the Rolanders on Tate Mountain. Every time we'd go up there, he'd announce, "The project for this weekend is a rock wall that we're going to build right here."

And we kids would go collecting rocks and build a wall.

Next time it was, "Let's go burn leaves!"

Today, I realize these projects were his way of spending time with us.

Daddy has a five-thousand-acre plantation—Woodhaven—outside Coolidge. He loves the place dearly but hardly relishes it as a "Gentleman's Plantation." It's a quail hunter's paradise, but he has a thousand projects going down there. That's what drives it. He'll wake up in the morning, look out the window, and say, "We need a lake right there!" And he'll start digging a lake. He's built outhouses and cabins.

No matter how successful, he'll always be the kid from Howell Mill Road, a staunch Republican with working-class roots and values. My grandfather didn't want either of his sons to go to college because he hadn't finished high school. He was afraid they'd get smarter than he was. "Nobody needs that college stuff; you need to go out and work," he'd grumble. Daddy did both.

Over the years, we children came to realize that for Daddy the bottom line is an absolute commitment to fairness. Charlie Loudermilk never looked down on anybody, ever. Though intensely focused on his business, he intuitively chose to do what was right and proved along the way that "You can do well by doing good."

Another of our family legends involves Daddy's and Ike Rolader's unlikely appearance at Martin Luther King's historic Selma-to-Montgomery civil rights march in March 1965. It turns out to be true. Well, mostly. At the time, Daddy was no crusader; he was just a struggling, small businessman trying to make ends meet. Ike had finished dental school at Emory University and opened his own practice. Both men needed whatever business they could grab and hang onto. "In those days," Daddy recalls, "it would not have been a popular thing to be connected to the black community in any way."

In any event, a call came in. I'll let my father pick up the rest of the story:

"Martin Luther King Jr.'s people (the Southern Christian Leadership Conference, SCLC) contacted me about renting some tents and chairs. Frank, the guy who ran our tent rental business was raised up in the mountains and was about as prejudiced as anybody I know. He came to me and told me what they wanted.

"I'd like to have the business," I told Frank. "And I think it's the right thing to do."

Frank looked at me funny. I told him, by the way, that any trouble he'd encounter over in Alabama would probably come from white people. "If you're going to handle it, you cannot get into any kind of problem, even if they spit in your face."

I also told Frank to rent a Hertz truck for the drive to Selma to keep the Aaron's name out of the public eye.

Two weeks earlier, on March 7, Alabama police, sheriffs' deputies, and mounted troopers had teargassed and beaten hundreds of voting-rights activists—most famously future congressman John Lewis—on the Edmund Pettus Bridge. Newsreels of "Bloody Sunday" had horrified the world and outraged

President Lyndon Johnson. Now Martin Luther King Jr. and thousands of civil rights supporters from around the country were massing for a second march on Montgomery, the state capital.

I couldn't help but notice that King's people paid for the tents and rental equipment in quarters, half-dollars, and rumpled dollar bills, scarce money obviously taken up in collections. They were working out of their back pockets. I knew the feeling.

When Frank and his crew arrived in Alabama, fifty Episcopal ministers volunteered to help him set up tents in a series of pastures along the fifty-odd mile route. "Hell, he doesn't need but two or three men," I told Ike at the time, "but they're part of the show."

On Saturday night March 20, Ike and I were in Atlanta having a drink or two out on the screened porch. Like almost everyone in the country, we were shocked by the violence taking place in Alabama; it was all further insult to the injury that the 1963 church bombings, Bull Connor, and the Birmingham riots had done to the state's good name. (That same week, President Johnson sent the landmark Voting Rights Act to Congress on the heels of the Voting Rights Act of 1964.)

Maybe the whiskey that night had something to do with it, but the next day, we decided to go over there and get in the middle of it. Our wives were worried about our safety, but when we hit the Jeff Davis Highway, the fifty-four-mile Selma-to-Montgomery route, it struck me that I was probably in the safest place in America.

To head off a repeat of Bloody Sunday, four thousand U.S. Army and National Guard troops had been mobilized, and they were lining the roads. U.S. District Judge Frank Johnson had given King and the marchers a green light, lifting a restraining order and ruling in favor of the black citizens' First Amendment rights to a protest march.

We parked along the road, and I walked up to some very tense Alabama State Patrol officers and asked them if they knew "where the tents were." Most of the troopers ignored us, and a couple had some nasty words, but finally one guy told us that the best way to find out where the tents were being pitched is to get up to the front of the march.

It wasn't a big deal. We were out in the country. We started walking and soon caught up. There were maybe six or eight marchers at the front of the line and a bunch of stragglers behind. I thought I'd ask Martin about the tents. I knew him a little bit. He was doing some of the marching. I didn't know Andy Young from Adam.

Ike and I got to the front line. I was about to ask Martin about my tents when I noticed a flatbed truck about twenty feet in front of us with a TV camera mounted on the back. It was moving at the same pace as we were, pointed at the leaders . . . and straight at us!

Ike looked up, saw that camera, and almost fainted. He was scared to death he'd wind up on television that night in Atlanta, and it'd look like he was marching. And he'd lose his whole dental practice, which he'd just built, and nobody would come to see him on Monday or ever again."

During the famous 1965 civil rights march from Selma to Montgomery, Alabama, representatives of Martin Luther King, Jr. contacted Charlie who made sure they had tents and chairs for the event.

Daddy always tells "the Martin Luther King story" with a laugh. Ike would always grin along. Daddy doesn't mention that he didn't bill Reverend King's group for the extra days they kept the tents and equipment. He does grumble that the SCLC didn't rent the stage upon which Martin Luther King gave his famous, "How Long? Not Long" speech from Aaron's. (The story is that Martin Luther King Jr., Joseph Lowery, Dean Martin, Nina Simone, Tony Bennett, and other notables were forced to stand on a makeshift stage constructed of planks supported by coffins borrowed from a Montgomery funeral parlor.

Many years later, when I asked my father why he got involved—foreshadowing of his support of Andy Young for mayor of Atlanta—he says "I didn't do a lot of thinking about it. When you were raised where I was, you pull for the underdog. Being an underdog, you relate to the underdog."

Maybe that's why the managers and employees at Aaron's feel on par with Charlie as human beings, i.e., "He doesn't treat me as inferior because I work in the mailroom." My father has been in their shoes and done much worse jobs. Today, he and Robin work closely together, and my brother is like my dad. He's grown up with the same values. As I mentioned, decades after the Selma march, Daddy was about the only white Atlanta businessman to support Andrew Young for mayor. He definitely took heat for that from his friends and business associates—our whole family did—but he never wavered. And time has proved him right.

Growing up, it was interesting to watch these two sides of Daddy in action. He sent me to private school against his own will. He'd spent all those summers at the Fritz Orr Camp with those wealthy children and had some definite opinions about the value of private school education. But Fritz was his absolute mentor and touchstone. So many years later, when Fritz told him, "Charlie, you need to send Lisa to Westminster," Daddy listened.

"Well, I don't send my children to private school," he replied. "I want them to go to public schools." They went round and round. Finally, he relented. "Okay if she tests well and she can get in, I'll send her." But he was never fully convinced this was what his children should be doing.

I suspect he joined the Cherokee Country Club because his mother convinced him he should. He does love playing golf with the boys. Then he got the notion that I should be a débutante. I didn't know what that was, but I responded, "Okay, I'll make my debut." They hold this ball at the Piedmont Driving Club, and all the girls have to wear white dresses. Mother and I went to Saks Fifth Avenue for the first time ever. This was 1976. We bought a dress that probably cost $400. We got home, and Daddy was upset at how much we spent.

"Wait a minute," I said. "you're the one telling me I should be a débutante. I didn't ask to be one!"

The truth is that some of the girls I met doing débutante stuff ended up being my friends for life. So Daddy was right. There's always been this push-pull with him. He doesn't want to spoil his kids, but he wants us to have everything he didn't have. He may give you a new car, but you dang better appreciate it.

My sister Linda, the youngest of us, came of age when Daddy was more successful. Success didn't change him. "We were asked to be at the top of society," she remembers with a laugh, "but Daddy expected us to buy our dresses at the discount place. He'd buy a hockey team, and we would scrimp. It was kind of confusing at the time, but today I understand it gave us the backbone to be successful in our own right. Not just successful. People see all three of Charlie's children as very genuine and relatable people. Daddy did a good job with that part, not raising rich kids."

Despite her incredible work ethic and the sacrifices she made, Granny Loudermilk was not a one-dimensional figure, a Mother Teresa of the Kitchen. She loved to giggle and laugh. She joked that Daddy, when he was born, was so cute that he was the ugliest girl she'd ever seen. (She'd been praying for a girl.) She had a warmth that drew people to her like a magnet. Her best friend was a woman named Sadie Vernoy. They'd get together every once in a while and go to dinner. If Granny didn't have a lot more

Charlie with his daughter Lisa at her formal début presentation—his dream, not hers!

friends, it was because she was working all the time. She and my mother, Mickey McQueen Loudermilk, were very close; they were closer, in fact, than Mickey was to her own mother. Mom became the daughter Addie Loudermilk never had.

Granny didn't take a lot of time off, but when she did, she loved to travel. She visited her sister Mary Surgeon in New York City once or twice. To her, that was the end-all and be-all. And she'd go on trips with us. I remember one time in Highlands, North Carolina, she and I were sharing a bedroom at the Highlands Inn. The walls were as thin as paper. We started laughing about something in the middle of the night. Granny was giggling and giggling. We woke up the entire floor.

She'd been deprived of her childhood—forced to care for her father, brother, and sister after her mother was hospitalized and later looked after her father's second wife, "Aunt Ida," who developed diabetes. I believe the little girl trapped inside her all those years got to come out when she was with her grandchildren. She was extremely sensitive about people and feelings.

Granny was a marvelous cook. She lived to be ninety-six and never considered not cooking with fatback. I have all of her cookbooks, written in her own hand. When my parents were out of town, we kids would stay at Granny and Jakus's house on Buford Highway and, later, on land they had in Sandy Springs. Buford Highway was almost rural back then, though their property was just a couple miles past Green's Liquor Store. At first, Jakus refused to move "way out there," but he got used to it. When he got up in the morning, he still had to have his Coca-Cola in a small glass bottle.

Jakus kept all these chickens and would wake us kids to feed them. Once, he took me to a cockfight with him in Demorest, his hometown. He wasn't fazed that I was the only girl in attendance. Usually, Jakus would take me to the stockyards on Howell Mill Road. As I recall, he was always promising to buy me a pony, but he never got around to it. He would hang out with his friends in front of an old, smelly kerosene stove and talk for hours. One time, when Robin and I were playing hide-and-seek in their house, we found a stack of his presents from Christmases past—still wrapped and unopened in his closet. Jakus was in his own world.

I remember a lovely creek running through the Sandy Springs property. Jakus and Granny kept a vegetable garden, more chickens, a fig tree, and abundant vines of muscadine and white scuppernong grapes. My sister, Linda, remembers being intoxicated by the scent of a giant gardenia bush that Granny grew near the house. "A perfume factory," in her imagination.

Granny and Jakus grew closer as they got older.

"Some people have to have a lot of romance in their lives," Linda recalled, standing in the clutter of her bustling design studio in California. "Trips, people, and parties. Neither Granny nor Jakus had to do that to be happy. They were satisfied to work their little farm. Though, she never stopped buzzing around, they lived a very sustainable life. Today, that's a choice people are so proud of. Back then, they just did it. That was quite a beautiful thing about them."

"My grandmother was courageous to let her entrepreneurial spirit free, as she tirelessly walked through challenges to create prosperity, in a time when women were not encouraged to work outside the home, let alone run a business."

—Linda Loudermilk

Part Three
Building a Business

"We never squeezed our customers to enhance the bottom line. Fairness is the bottom line."

—Charlie Loudermilk
on the early years

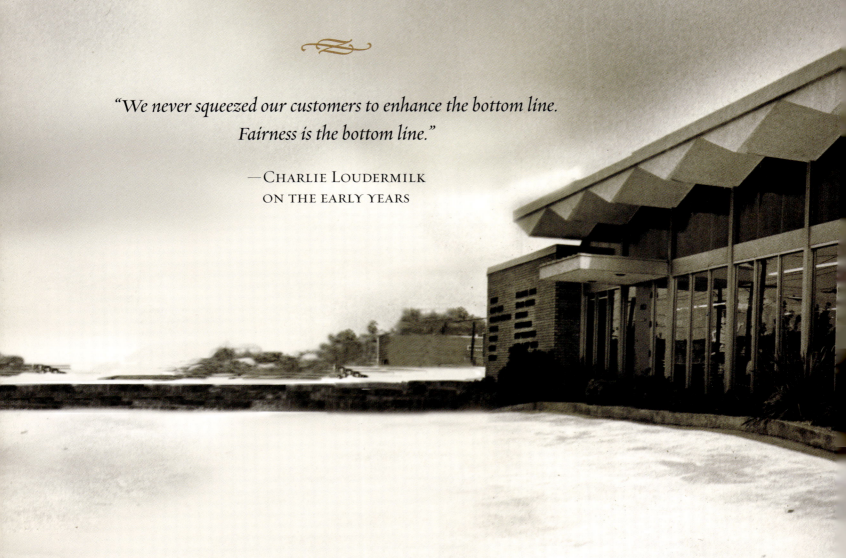

Chapter Eleven

"We were always fighting to buy something to rent."
— Charlie Loudermilk on Aaron's early days

While working for Pfizer in Greensboro, North Carolina, I lived in a rooming house, an arrangement typical of the times and my limited resources. I don't want to make too much of coincidence, but the lady who ran the place had a son-in-law who owned Owenby Rental, a business that instantly intrigued me. Owenby rented party and sick room equipment. I realized that, like death and taxes, parties and sick rooms are two inescapable and repetitive aspects of everyday life. I filed the idea away in my brain and, as I've described, continued climbing up the ladder at Pfizer.

I kept thinking about this rental business after I returned to Atlanta to run the Rose Bowl II restaurant with Mother. I remember seeing an article in the *Saturday Evening Post* on Abbey Rents, a west coast company that rented a whole range of party items: glassware, silverware, tents and stages, chairs, tables . . . you name it. In America, as you know, trends typically start in California and march relentlessly eastward.

In simple terms, the notion of inventory that could go out into the marketplace and continue to generate revenue long after its initial cost had been recouped seemed too good to be true. (It was.) I imagined an army of sparkling glasses, crystal punch bowls, and shiny spoons and forks marching alongside me on the yellow brick road to becoming a millionaire. As I would learn in the years ahead, to my despair, such a business required constant infusions of fresh capital.

I could raise maybe $500 bucks.

Once again, Ike Rolader plays a part in the story. After his father had passed away, Ike was very concerned about his mother's well-being. Buena Rolader—always Miz Rolader to me—had a head for

Opposite: Charlie Loudermilk—born entrepreneur.

business. I said to Ike, "I'm going to start a rental company, and your mother can run it." So I placed an ad in the Yellow Pages. As I've said many times, our corporate name, "Aaron's," is directly traceable to its alphabetical prominence in these listings. Loudermilk Rentals has a certain ring to it, but I figured we'd have been too far down the page.

When I saw that *Saturday Evening Post* article I thought, "I've got to get into the phone book ahead of Abbey Rents. They weren't in Atlanta yet, but they were moving east. I started thinking of names. It sounds crazy, but I settled on *Abbet Rents* because the name would come before *Abbey Rents*.

Well, Abbey Rents heard about us some way, and, sure enough, their lawyers contacted me. My old buddy, Tom Shelton, (Yale Law, 1951), was now my lawyer at Kilpatrick, Cody, Rogers, McClatchey & Regenstein. He advised me that I could probably win a lawsuit, but since I was so new, why not change the name. "Aaron's" filled the bill (two A's!) but I covered my bet by starting another company I named "AAA Rentals." That one didn't last long.

My first outlet was a little store on Peachtree Road and Peachtree Battle next to Fred's Fruit Emporium, a hangout where in the summer, teenagers would buy slices of chilled watermelon. I eventually bought a used truck and hired William Strange to drive it. Miz Rolader and William Strange were my first two employees. I got a hold of an Abbey Rents catalog somewhere and told Miz Rolader, "Everything in there, we'll rent!"

"What do I charge?" she asked sensibly.

"Oh?" I thought for a minute. "You're the businesswoman. How about 10 percent of cost?" We spent the next weeks developing our own pricing scheme.

I went back to work at the Rose Bowl. Miz Rolader manned the phones. She stayed with me fifteen years, booking our orders. We had a great time together. She liked to claim she was "the mother of the rental business." She passed away. As did Ike, and a lot of my old friends and colleagues.

I've described the first Aaron's sale many times over the years. In the summer of 1955, I booked three hundred folding chairs to be rented for three days at the cost of a dime a day per chair—at the time, less than the price of an eight-ounce bottle of Coca-Cola. I ran out and purchased some very used army surplus chairs. The rental order came from a man named Kickliner who was in the auction and antique business. He was holding an estate sale at a big house on the corner of Woodhaven Road and West Paces Ferry Road.

I started with a partner, a guy we called "Red" Jewell. After that long day delivering those chairs in the hot sun and then picking them up for the grand sum of $90.00, Red decided he wanted out of this business. I had to scrape up the money to buy him out. For years, Red went around town saying he used to "own half of Aaron Rents."

As I've mentioned, my main competition at the time came from the funeral parlors. They had lots of down time and lots of chairs and tents on hand and would happily loan them. Another of our regular

Aaron's first rental chair—the icon of an empire.

customers at the Rose Bowl was H.M. "Fred" Patterson who operated a busy funeral home (today, H.M. Patterson & Son) at 1020 Spring Street. Every day, Fred came in for lunch with his brother-in-law at exactly three minutes before noon. He sat at the same table and ordered the same thing from the same waitress, Lucille, who knew he wanted his bread toasted almost black. Like most of our regulars, Fred loved Addie. I kept trying to talk him out of loaning his chairs and letting me rent them. He finally agreed.

Today, my surviving old friends joke that I shanghaied them into helping me wash the dirty dishes, load trucks, and move equipment. I honestly don't remember a lot of that. I do remember the time Ike and I delivered a huge load of chairs to the Rural Electric Association for their annual meeting. We had to unload them and load them back up when the meeting was over. And unload them again in our warehouse. Ike moaned about that one job for the next forty years. Later, I'll mention some of the benefits he derived from his association with Aaron's. I ended up wrecking my knees just as mother had in the restaurants. It was brutal work, but it had to be done.

I'd noticed something with that very first order . . . how the ringing phones kept Miz Rolader scribbling orders all day, Billy Strange making deliveries, and, later, in the waves of repeat customers. I guess I saw it in my wife's eyes when I came home late for supper every single night and in my young children's faces when all I could talk about was growing my company. It was something every small businessman and Fortune 500 CEO craves more than anything else.

Demand.

In fact, I almost drowned in an ocean of opportunity. The dilemma, in a nutshell, was all this demand for my products and no capital or financing to expand and replace my inventory. You know me pretty well by now. You can bet I *hated* to turn down business that I'd worked like hell to get. I had spent scarce money to get the phone to ring, and then couldn't service customers? And, I worried, if I didn't serve them well, they would not use me again, and then tell all of their friends not to use me. It quickly became a vicious circle like those whirlpools that carried so many doughty sailors to their graves.

Unlike Mother, who knew how to run restaurants, I had to learn the peculiarities of my business on the fly. In retail, for example, you buy an item for a dollar and sell it for $1.99. You take your profit and reinvest it. In rental, you buy an item for a dollar and you make ten cents on the first rental, ten cents on the second, and so on. It takes a long time to recoup your initial investment. Buy an item, and it doesn't rent, don't buy a second. Don't buy a million dollars' worth of inventory and three airplanes on spec and *then* try to rent them. I didn't do that. I did start a tool rental business but soon found that a smelly lawn mower didn't belong in a showroom alongside a silver punch bowl. The most challenging and disheartening truth about the rental business is that you need capital—lots of it—to generate significant cash flow.

At first, I focused on party rentals and worked with caterers. We'd provide the china, silverware, punch bowls, tablecloths, silver candelabra, and chafing dishes. We'd set up, and the caterers would truck in the food and beverages. It was good business and generated many referrals.

I quickly outgrew the store at Peachtree Battle and then moved to 499 Peachtree Street across from the Medical Arts Building. At that point, I'd gotten into renting sickroom equipment, and we began a very rapid expansion. Suddenly my warehouse was piled to the rafters with equipment. Somehow, my three hundred folding chairs had grown to ten thousand, and, in addition, we had three thousand tables, and hundreds of hospital beds and wheelchairs. Aaron's had maybe ten employees.

You've heard me go on and on about "people skills." I'd learned valuable lessons as a salesman, and they were reinforced working in the restaurants. Now, in the rental business, the most important was pleasing people. Pleasing five hundred people was second nature to Mother; she'd get upset if one person complained about the food or service. This became second nature to me. I'd deliver hospital beds, wheelchairs, and everything else. I'd even put people in traction. These were the days before malpractice suits also became second nature to Americans. Sure, I could have had someone else do it, but I got a kick out delivering such personal service.

Mother and I—she was a full partner in Aaron's—pulled every dollar we could from the Rose Bowls. The restaurants now generated about $500 a day, but Aaron's was terribly undercapitalized. I was constantly rushing in and out of the Sears & Roebuck store on West Paces Ferry Road and other wholesalers on the south side of town, having to pay retail prices every time a customer wanted something we didn't stock and then hoping the deposits I made into my account (or more likely, moved from my personal account to the restaurant account to Aaron's account), would clear before my checks bounced.

This was a time when the banker knew your name *and* your standing the minute you walked in the door. A time when it took three or four days for a check to go through. I was playing that game, trying to pay suppliers for everything from silver candelabras to wheelchairs, and furniture, pulling money out of the air like a cheap magician. The friendly neighborhood banker may have disappeared without a trace, but the phrase for what I was doing hasn't changed much: "kiting checks."

Before long, I didn't have the best reputation in the world for paying bills. And it galled me. Too many times, I had to stand, hat-in-hand, trying to borrow money to grow my company, having to explain that the rental business *was not a gamble*. If anything, I was scrambling to keep up with demand.

"Charlie, you know we're not going to lend you money on used tables and chairs . . ." the bankers would lecture.

I'd stand there squirming like a schoolboy being disciplined.

"How are we going to get our money on an old wheelchair if you go belly-up?"

I wanted to drag my bankers over to my little office and let them hear the phone ringing and talk to the customers I was scrambling to satisfy. Bankers didn't work that way—and still don't.

The bottom line was that old Jeep had gotten himself into a business he never should have been in the first place. That's my story in a nutshell. Remember, I had to borrow that original $500 to even get going. If I had been somebody with a Buckhead background and family dollars, I believe I would have had a much, much easier time making a good idea work. At the time, I felt very bitter. I had a hell of a problem.

The day came when I walked into Trust Company of Georgia, the bank that had originally lent us the money—with Tubby Davis of Davis Brothers Cafeteria as a cosigner—to get Rose Bowl II up and running. We kept our accounts with them. Imagine how I felt when I walked in and they told me they didn't want to do business with me anymore. I kept switching money from one account to another, betting on the "float." It was a tough, tough deal. I moved our meager accounts over to the Fulton National Bank.

I've thought about that day a lot. Frankly, if I'd known going in, the price I would pay—physically and emotionally—and the stress I endured and visited upon my mother and family, I would never have gone into the rental business. There were days when I would have given the company away if I could have just walked away and tried something—anything—else.

Today, I see the bankers' point. I had zero collateral, just a bunch of used chairs and forks and spoons. The bitter medicine they made me swallow is probably the reason I'm here today. If I had been given all the money I thought I needed, I would have definitely outgrown my ability to stay on top of the business.

Here, again, Mother sustained me, not just with her absolute commitment to me, but by the example she set. As hard as I worked, she'd worked harder. And if I really stepped back, I could discern

Drowning in success, Aaron's quickly expanded to a second store on Buford Highway (opposite) and a third store on the corner of West Peachtree and 14th Street (above).

that she was living the American Dream; in one generation she had gone from a house with outdoor plumbing to watching her sons graduate from college. Of course, she was never one to taste its fruits. She prepared the meal and set the table for us. Here I was in my thirties, and I still needed her by my side. I guess it was the years as a boy I'd spent scrambling for nickels and dimes, that kept me going these first, brutal years. Maybe it was an entrepreneurial gene I'd inherited from Mother. I'm convinced entrepreneurs are born with a special drive. A hunger. She sure had it.

Chapter Twelve

"We ain't had any furniture."

—Frank Reece,
Aaron's tent man

In any event, the Rose Bowl restaurants kept Aaron's going for five years. In those days, I spent 80 percent of my time in the restaurants. First I'd run down to Pershing Point before 11:30 A.M., get everyone seated for lunch, get 'em served, and clean the tables. Then I'd rush back to Aaron's around 2:00 P.M., work all afternoon, and return to the restaurant for the evening dinner rush. Many nights, after the restaurant closed, buzzing with excess energy, I'd drive around Atlanta scouting locations for new stores. I was dreaming big dreams.

Two fellows who ran a loan office out of a Macon hotel provided my first real financing. That deal was handled by my good friend, Jack Wall, an investment banker with Merrill Lynch and my attorney, frat brother, and lifelong friend, Tom Shelton. (You may remember that it was Tom's father, Charles D. Shelton, who persuaded Fritz Orr to open his first after-school camp in Shelton's Buckhead backyard.) It was a good thing I had such legal and financial firepower with me because I would have signed *any note* anyone stuck in front of me. I remember the terms, $300,000 with one percent a month, plus options on our stock should we go public. For years, Tom Shelton recognizing my precarious position, declined to send me a bill for his services.

The money lasted a year or two. Aaron's revenue, along with our debt, had begun to snowball. We could barely keep up with our growth. Remember, a *healthy* rental company has higher and higher debt because cash flow doesn't pay for growth. If you grow at 20 percent a year; your cash flow may be 15 percent. So you have to borrow that five percent or start sinking.

Finally, the gods began to smile in my favor. In 1965, the U.S. Air Force awarded Lockheed-Georgia the contract to manufacture the prop jet-engined C-5A Galaxy transport, a flying behemoth with

Opposite: Charlie Loudermilk with a few of Aaron's early top executives—"mad men" of the rental industry!

a ninety-ton payload. The multiyear contract had an immediate "trickle down" effect on the local Atlanta economy all the way to my struggling company on Buford Highway. A similar spike had occurred when Marietta Bell's wartime B-29 plant generated hundreds of jobs. (During World War II the Roladers made a living patching worn-out tires for workers commuting up and down what is now Cobb Parkway to Marietta.)

Lockheed's job shoppers began a nationwide search for draftsmen, engineers, welders, electricians, crane operators, and the whole gamut of well-paid workers required to get a new aircraft off the ground. Lockheed employees soon overflowed the available apartments in Marietta, most of which were unfurnished. They started showing up at Aaron's looking to rent bedroom and living room suites, tables lamps—you name it. The problem, as my tent man, Frank, might have put it, "We ain't had any furniture."

The influx of skilled workers triggered a microcosm for what was stirring in Atlanta, and to a greater or lesser degree, throughout the South and West. We were not yet the Sunbelt, but the great migration of people, ideas, and capital from the small towns of the South and crowded cities of the Rust Belt that would transform the region over the next decades was underway. Atlanta would unquestionably become the "buckle of the Sunbelt," but, at first, we faced stiff competition from Birmingham with its steel mills, as well as from commercial and manufacturing centers such as Memphis, Nashville, and Chattanooga. Birmingham's hopes vanished in the aftermath of Bull Connor's police dogs and fire hoses, the bombing of the 16th Street Baptist Church, and the ensuing negative images that were broadcast all over the world. For that moment on, if you were a Fortune 500 company or an overseas company looking to establish a regional headquarters, Birmingham would have been a very hard sell.

Atlanta was home to Martin Luther King Jr. and the Southern Christian Leadership Conference. The city had been spared violent racial unrest since the first decades of the twentieth century. This was no accident. Atlanta had a vibrant, upwardly mobile African-American middle class centered around Auburn Avenue. Its historically black colleges—Morehouse, Spelman, Clark University, Morris Brown—had been churning out a professional and leadership class for more than a century. Among them, the civil rights activist, John Wesley Dobbs, Maynard Jackson's grandfather, was probably the best known.

The white business community, prodded by Citizens and Southern National Bank president Mills B. Lane and visionary mayors like William Hartsfield and Ivan Allen, saw the civil rights movement as inevitable. They worked behind-the-scenes to assure the shift to black political power would be peaceable. They decided the business of Atlanta would be business, not race-baiting. We became the "City Too Busy to Hate." I am humbled to say I played a small part in these momentous events, but that would come much later.

At the time, I was confounded trying to get beds, tables, and chairs into the hands of all those flush Lockheed workers. I was also seeing demand from college graduates just entering the Atlanta job market, part of a flood tide of young people fleeing small towns for the excitement and opportunities of the big city. Together, they would form the vanguard of the swinging singles scene that would soon be known as "Hotlanta."

I still remember our first furniture rental. By 1963, Aaron's had expanded to perhaps two or three stores. Four young women came in to rent furniture for their new apartment. They were college grads working new jobs. They rented four twin beds, which was all they could afford. Frank Reece and I delivered the beds personally in my station wagon. We even brought a celebratory six-pack of beer. The apartment, on Peachtree Hills Avenue, was a tiny two-bedroom, one bath walk-up. Ironically, one of the girls, Margie Stockton, later went into real estate and did extremely well. Over the years, I would buy three houses from her. It's funny how life circles around on itself.

I saw furniture rental as the future for Aaron's. The problem was the furniture industry, which was centered in places like Hickory, North Carolina, was firmly rooted in the slow-moving past. Typically, I'd order one hundred suites of furniture in August, only to be told that the run on that particular line wouldn't take place until November. For three months, I'd have to sit there, my showroom bare, turning customers away. At one point, the only things Aaron's could deliver were lamps and mattresses.

I couldn't live with that. I'm the guy who needs to control everything that affects my future. So, my first acquisition was a small mattress manufacturing plant on Buford Highway, right here in town. Then I partnered with an upholstery operation in Hickory. It was the right move at the right time. As Bear Bryant used to say, "Luck is preparation meeting opportunity." Today, our MacTavish Furniture Industries operates ten factories in four states, manufacturing nearly half of Aaron's furniture, as well as mattresses and home accessories. We'd never get caught flatfooted again.

Demand for furniture was so robust that I ran around picking fabrics myself. Today, everyone laughs at the plaids and other unfortunate patterns I slapped on cushions, sofas, and chairs. They rented because nobody had anything else to offer. Furniture became the driver. Everything else took a backseat. Before long, I sold off the tent rental and party and sick room supply businesses. I was starting to breathe a little easier.

My $300,000 loan was settled and replaced by a $1,000,000 loan from the Life Insurance Company of Georgia, a major lender at the time. Life of Georgia's executive vice president (later president and CEO) was my friend and fellow Chi Phi, Rankin Smith, who famously purchased the Atlanta Falcons for $8.5 million in 1965. His son, Taylor, sold the franchise twenty-five years later to Home Depot cofounder Arthur Blank for $545 million, certainly one of the deals of the century.

Rankin, who passed away in 1997, was a complicated man. A child of privilege, he grew up in Buckhead, attended North Fulton High School and the University of Georgia before being handed the reins of the family business. Despite these blessings, I suspect, like so many of the boys I'd met at Fritz Orr's camp, Rankin had a difficult time relating to ordinary people. I know he would have loved to sit down on a park bench and start talking to some stranger or share a chew of tobacco with him. He just could not do it. Rankin was the sweetest, nicest guy in the world until he had a few

drinks; then he could be insensitive, and at times, downright mean.

A day came when Miz Rolader signaled to me that Rankin Smith was on the line. Rankin told me we needed to have a meeting. When your banker calls it's rarely a good omen.

"Charlie, my office or yours?"

"Mine," I told him.

Life of Georgia's headquarters was an imposing limestone edifice on West Peachtree Street. I still operated out of a store on 14th Street.

Rankin showed up and got right to the point.

"Charlie, we don't think you need any more money."

I was disappointed, but, fortunately, I was not unprepared. If this was a tennis game it would have

been a volley I smashed at his head. I told Rankin that I'd already secured an $8 million line of credit from General Electric Credit Corporation (GECC).

He was shocked. "I hope those Yankee bastards treat you as well as we've treated you!" he spluttered and stormed out.

The next day, we were friends again. That was Rankin. We stayed buddies for the rest of his life, but the man could wear you out.

Aaron's furniture rentals expanded from individual consumers like Margie Stockton to corporate clients—office managers, property managers offering furnished apartments, extended stay hotels, and other kinds of short term housing. Our business model evolved from flogging 10-cent-a-day folding chairs to a streamlined, high-volume, low-margin operation.

It sounds like an oxymoron, but I'm a workaholic who enjoys himself. Enjoyment and hard work are not mutually exclusive. I *love* getting phone calls. Friends and family often advise me to turn my cell phone off ("It's eight o'clock!"), but I like talking to people. I also like solving problems (and get frustrated when I can't). Mother was the same way. (Remember what I said about one dissatisfied diner out of a thousand causing her distress?)

Growing up, I was always aware of a larger world beyond the circumscribed borders of our neighborhood. I wanted to be a part of things, but I didn't know how, except by working hard, always staying on the alert for opportunity, and noticing things that maybe others missed. I am not talking about just discarded Coca-Cola bottles exchanged for a one cent deposit but, rather, about big picture things: how people treated one another; who was honest, hypocritical, decent, or cruel; who worked hard and who didn't. It's easy to see such things when you're the outsider trying to get in.

I am no longer an outsider. Aaron's revenues this year are estimated to reach $3 billion. With success comes responsibility. My son Robin, Aaron's CEO, and I fight to stay focused on what's important. We're never so busy that we disregard our employees' dignity or needs, and we're never so pressured that we forget to make sure that they are enjoying themselves and seeing the same opportunities I did so many years ago.

Today, everything moves so much faster—technology plays a big part in that. Often the issue is finding enough hours in the day to do it all. Maybe we don't do the physical work our parents did, but mental work is more tiring than physical work. Dig a ditch for your eight hours and go home. You don't worry about that ditch until tomorrow. You don't worry about anything. In the business world, you never can leave it all behind. With cell phones, BlackBerrys, and everything else, you are never out of the picture.

At Aaron's, we try to strike a balance between hard work and play. It's fundamental to our culture and, I believe, typical of our employees. I don't have to look any further than Ken Butler to illustrate my point. Like many of Aaron's senior managers, Ken moved up the ladder from an entry-level job to become our chief operating officer. He's been with the company more than thirty years—after what he describes a "rocky start." He worked at one of our first stores, off I-85 near what is now Spaghetti Junction. Asked to relate some of his early experiences working with Aaron's, Ken recalled:

A lot of us at Aaron's had played sports in school, and we were drawn to any kind of competition. One weekend, a few of us challenged a competitor, General Furniture Leasing, to a flag football game on Sunday. Simple and friendly enough. Well, we were running some warm-up plays—I was a running back—and the quarterback handed the ball off to me. Bam! One of my own teammates tackled me! You're supposed to pull the flag! My legs went up in the air, and my knee went "pop" and all sideways. As it turned out, I'd torn my ligaments and broken my leg. I had to have surgery and ended up with a cast up to my hip.

Charlie and Robin work hard to remind everyone that they are more than employees at Aaron's, they truly are family. Company picnics, gatherings, and NASCAR events are just a few ways they balance work with fun.

At the time, I'd been with the company about four years and was recently married. You didn't miss work. No question; Charlie expected you back ASAP. One morning, a few weeks after my accident, I'd just finished loading the trucks for our daily deliveries when a UPS truck arrived to drop off some cocktail and end tables. I was hobbling around and asked the driver to help me. I had this broken leg, my crew was out, and I didn't have any help.

We got the tables off the truck. By then, I was worn out, so I figured I'd set them up in the showroom later. It was a Wednesday, a slow day. All I had was a bookkeeper in the store. Suddenly, I saw this Oldsmobile whirl into a parking space in front of the building. It was Charlie. Oh, hell! He got out of the car, walked into the store, and stomped around the showroom. Instead of praising my valiant efforts to get to work, he chewed my butt out because there was a hole on the floor. A couch had been removed that morning by our delivery guys, and the "hole" had not been filled in.

In Charlie's world, a hole is a mortal sin.

Charlie gave me zero sympathy about my broken leg. He didn't even see my leg. I got a long lesson about being a merchant and never having a hole on the floor. Then he looked around suspiciously.

"Where are the new cocktail and end tables that got shipped here today? They did get here, didn't they Ken?"

"Yes, sir," I stammered. "I've got them in the back."

"In the back! The next customer who comes in the door might want a cocktail and end table!"

"Yes, sir."

I started to make excuses about my leg and then decided to shut up and swallow my medicine. Today, you will never see a hole in any Aaron's store. It became a policy, part of our culture, and it makes perfectly good sense. One of the building blocks of our business model is Respect the Consumer. Think about walking into a grocery store and seeing a couple of boxes of cereal on an empty shelf. The first thing you'll think is "This is old stuff. I've missed all the good stuff. I'm going somewhere else."

I made a lot of mistakes in those days. I probably could have gotten fired three times because I didn't know any better, but I survived. I look back and say maybe I was right 50 percent and wrong half the time. I got better because Charlie allowed me to learn from my mistakes.

It's easier to recall the fun stuff. In the seventies, as Charlie mentioned, Atlanta had lots of apartment communities. Ninety-nine percent of our customers were apartment dwellers, typically young singles, students, or married couples who needed fill-in furniture, and the occasional snowbird who never made it to Florida. Most didn't know if they were going to be here for a year or longer so they hesitated to put down roots.

Aaron's marketed directly to apartment managers hoping to generate referrals. A pool party was about as sophisticated as we got. Local liquor distributors would provide rum, kegs of beer, hats, and other stuff in return for promoting their brands. Imagine a happy hour where drinks were free and you didn't have to drive home. By far, the most popular item was an Aaron's T-shirt that read, "We lease by the piece."

Of course, that led to our wet T-shirt contests.

I'd have remind myself, "I'm getting paid to do this!"

All these years later, I still am.

I don't want to make too much of our struggles. Overcoming hardships and beating the odds is, after all, the quintessential path to success. I followed a path others had blazed before me, and making your way up the ladder is the American Dream. Working with my mother and building Aaron's was, in so many ways, a joy beyond measure. We complemented each other; we strove to maintain the human touch, not as an advertising slogan, but because it is the essence of a well-lived life. We insisted always on fairness. We never saw customers, who were often struggling to obtain the basic necessities, as sponges to be squeezed and tossed away to enhance the bottom line.

Fairness is the bottom line.

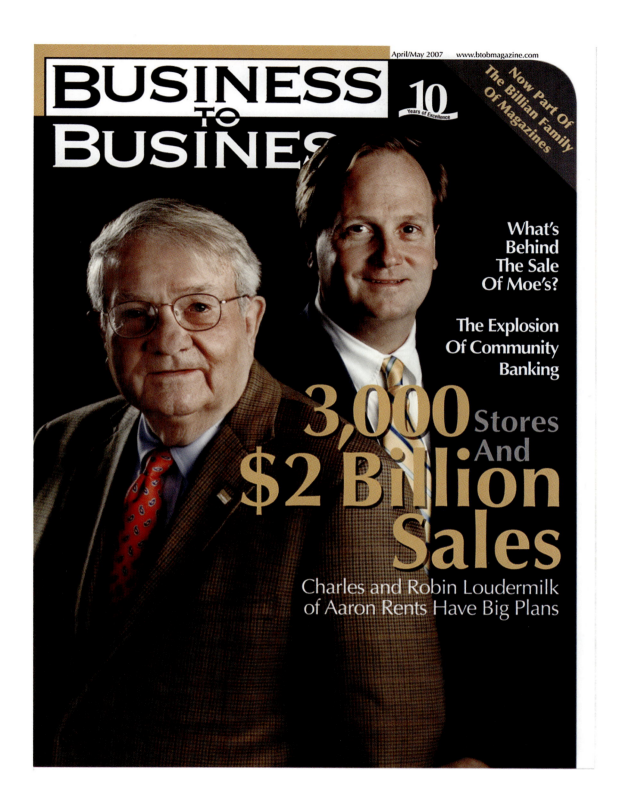

Chapter Thirteen

"You get to my age, you ask yourself, 'What is life?'
When all is said and done, it's two things:
family and friends."

— Charlie Loudermilk at eighty-three

Sometime in the early 1970s, I decided to go dove hunting in Mexico with some of my good buddies. I'd hunted and fished and played poker with these guys most of my adult life. Rankin Smith was part of the group, as was Dan Shepherd, and the well-known developers and community leaders, Paul Duke and John Aderhold. Dan, whose family founded the Shepherd Construction Company and, later, the Shepherd Center, and I talked to twice a day for thirty years. Dan, Rankin, and Paul have since passed away. Outliving most of your peers is one of life's bittersweet possibilities.

Three of us, Duke, Aderhold, and I, brought our sons along. I was hoping for a real father-son adventure with Robin. We traveled in three planes—Rankin Smith's, Dan Shepherd's, and a plane on loan to us from a contractor in Gainesville, Georgia, whose name I can't recall. The plan was to fly into McAllen, Texas, a few miles from the Rio Grande and then make our way into Mexico. The area on both sides of the border is renowned for its abundant game—duck, quail, and doves. Deer-hunting didn't appeal to me at all. After my father had me shoot the family hog between the eyes with a .22 rifle when I was a boy, I've never, ever hunted anything but birds.

Robin and I traveled in the borrowed plane—a top-of-the-line Aero-Commander—a business aircraft that could accommodate as many as seven passengers. Our pilot was Neil Ferguson, a skilled veteran who'd flown bombers in the European theater in World War II.

John Aderhold, Paul Duke, and his son, Paul Jr., were with us on the plane. Our flight plan was to stop in Auburn, Alabama, to pick up Tommy Aderhold, fly across Louisiana, and then, after a fuel stop

Opposite: Charlie Loudermilk loves nature, horses, and hunting birds, almost as much as building his business.

in Lake Charles, continue down into Texas. The Aero-Commander is a high-wing design so its belly sits lower than its propellers—a feature that would soon take on critical importance.

Over Lake Charles, what had been a routine flight went way wrong. From the cockpit, Ferguson announced that our retractable landing gear was malfunctioning. Rather than the "three green" signal indicating the wheels were locked in landing position, a warning light in the cockpit glowed red. The wheels were dangling like a marionette's legs under the plane.

Ferguson blew the nitrogen bottles, a one-shot emergency system designed to use compressed nitrogen stored in four bottles to literally blow the landing gear into its "locked" position. That failed, as did a steep dive in which the pilot attempted to use gravity to the same purpose. We were forced to attempt a wheels-dangling, belly-landing without brakes to slow the plane once we hit the ground. Such a landing—aluminum skin screeching and sparking on the tarmac—could easily send us cart-wheeling out of control and trigger a fire and explosion.

I looked at Robin. He was twelve years old, sitting behind me next to Paul Duke. He nodded attentively as he listened to the pilot radio our situation to the control tower. Ferguson had spotted a narrow strip of grass between the two concrete runways. He circled a few times scanning the strip for rocks, depressions or unseen ditches that could flip the hurtling plane over.

Tommy Aderhold was in the right seat. His job was to throw the switches killing the engines the moment we touched down. I was to position myself by the cabin door, throw it open the second the plane hit the ground to keep it from jamming, and then assist everyone in evacuating the craft as soon as we came to a stop. Below, I watched the fire trucks and emergency rescue vehicles, lights flashing, lining up along the runway.

"Have I killed my own son?" I couldn't shake the terrible thought from my head.

As Ferguson lined up the plane to begin his approach, I turned to Paul Duke, who was a former professional football player and an All-American center at Georgia Tech.

"Paul, if you come out without Robin, I'll kill you," I blurted.

To his credit, Paul ignored me.

"I've done this before in France during the war," Ferguson announced calmly. He had been captain of a B-52 bomber at the age of only 19. "If all goes well, we just tear up a bunch of antennas underneath the plane. The man was a masterful pilot, completely in control of the situation as we descended into harm's way.

Bam!

Moments later, we hit the ground. Ferguson fought to hold us steady as the runaway airplane shrieked down the grassy strip. Unfortunately, Tommy threw the kill switches the wrong away and fuel kept pumping into the engines. Just then, as I threw open the door, a gust of wind caught the left wing, driving the right wing into the ground. The propeller was spinning madly. We couldn't get out at that point! The prop began tearing up the ground and then caught fire. We skidded 1,300 feet before coming to a stop. Somehow we got out, evacuating as the rescue teams roared up.

Robin and I kissed the ground. When I caught my breath and stopped shaking, I told Ferguson, "Your expertise saved our lives. If the day comes that you ever need a job, I'll have a job for you."

We spent the rest of the afternoon in the airport manager's office. Later, Rankin sent his plane to pick us up, and we continued on our way without incident, though I didn't have much stomach for killing birds.

Years later, Ferguson called saying he needed a job because his boss had sold his plane. At the time, Dan Shepherd and I had gone halves on an airplane, and we had pilots under contact. They gracefully resigned after I explained the promise I had made.

You bet I kept my promise. A deal is a deal.

Going through trauma always makes you draw closer to those you love, though, once again, I can't explain exactly why in words. When my daughter Linda was a young girl she suffered terribly from acute bouts of asthma. She was constantly on powerful steroids and other medications and was forever fighting for an easy breath—something the rest of us take for granted. On one occasion, her condition grew so serious that we rushed her to the Piedmont Hospital Emergency Room.

She'd developed pneumonia. The desperate physicians used what must have been a mechanical ventilator to force air to open the airways in her lungs. It was so powerful that the blast ruptured one of her lungs. I stood there watching as my little daughter's hands and feet turned blue from oxygen deprivation.

"Daddy, am I going to die?" she gasped.

"No," I managed. "You're a fighter. You'll make it. Hang in there!"

I wasn't so sure. I left the room and cried like a baby for some time.

One of the doctors was forced to make an incision to reinflate her lung. Hopefully the hole would seal like a patch on a tire tube. The procedure worked. I made my way out into the hall. So many of our friends were gathered there. For the first time in my life, I couldn't stop crying. This was so unlike me.

Six weeks later, Linda set a track record at The Westminster School. The girl is a fighter.

On that runway in Lake Charles, my heart felt like it would burst, not with the residue of terror or whatever massive dose of adrenalin was pumping through me, but love. Love for Robin and my daughters, for all fathers and their sons and daughters. And mostly for this incredible gift we too often take for granted or devalue or ignore . . . our family.

I would like to say the experience changed my life overnight, like the New Testament's Saul struck from his horse on the road to Tarsus and transformed into Saint Paul. I was still chasing my dreams full speed, but I resolved to be a better man, a better son to Addie, and a better father. I didn't always succeed. But at eighty-three years old, I'm still working to keep that promise.

Ironically, it was my brother Jim who'd die in an airplane crash. I've mentioned Jim was a Georgia Tech grad, an aeronautical engineer, and a man meticulous in everything he did. He was also a hell of a pilot who owned three airplanes including the Beechcraft Baron he was flying on the day he died. After his stint in the navy, Jim traveled, working for Texaco and then selling cable. He also worked with me for a while before finally relocating to Pensacola, Florida, where, with money from Mother, he purchased a terminal that served as a port for fuel barges plying the Gulf of Mexico.

When Jim was at Georgia Tech, he wanted to join a fraternity. As I mentioned, he'd been turned down by the two best groups on campus, mainly because no one knew who he was. (Fulton County High School graduates were rare at Georgia Tech.) He took it pretty badly. One of Mother's suppliers, a man who'd been a member of a fraternity at Georgia Tech told her he could get Jim into Phi Kappa Phi. Now the question became, "How do we get the money to pay his initiation fee?" Well, someone else had asked Mother about putting on a Maids Night Out supper at the First Presbyterian Church on Peachtree Street.

In those days, all the maids in Buckhead had Thursday nights off. On top of her other work, Mom took the job of serving supper to the church members who had requested it in order to raise money for Jim's fees. Dog-tired after a long day, she rode the streetcar to the church. This is who she was.

Jim was an entrepreneur, changing businesses like other men change shirts. He owned an electrical contracting business, a salvage business, and a handful of self-service garages. Eventually, I brought him in as a partner, which was a dream come true for my mother. Jim was supposed to open the first Aaron's store in Birmingham, Alabama. Granted, it wasn't much to inspire confidence, just an old, rehabbed gas station. Unfortunately, Jim proved more interested in partying than party rentals. The store tanked, and I was livid. Needless to say, our partnership petered out.

Jim never had children, and, for some reason, his wife disliked my mother. Mother would reach out to her, send her birthday presents and everything else, but the woman would never respond. It broke her heart. Still, whatever his faults, Jim would call home every Sunday night. I still remember how much Mother looked forward to getting that call.

On the morning of Friday, February 2, 1990, Jim and a friend, Florida Circuit Court Judge Clyde Wells, took off from Pensacola Regional Airport also bound for Lake Charles. They were going hunting—Jim loved hunting quail and ducks and dove—and had their birddogs with them. Five minutes into the flight, the twin-engine Beechcraft with Jim at the controls, plunged to earth in a residential neighborhood, exploded, and burned. The first reports mention heavy fog, mechanical difficulties, and an attempt to head back to the airport. However, the Federal Aviation Administration investigation into the crash determined that the yoke—used to control the plane's "attitude," i.e., pitch and roll—had been shifted to Judge Wells' position. It's likely that Jim suffered either a heart attack or stroke and the desperate judge took the controls and ran the plane straight into the ground.

Jim suffered from very high blood pressure and apparently wasn't taking his medications. He had a doctor friend up in Marietta who would certify him fit to fly, a wink and a nod that maybe cost my sixty-five-year-old brother his life. My father had passed away before Jim was killed. I was terrified that Mother, now almost ninety, would hear of Jim's death before I could break the news to her. In the end, she didn't take his passing nearly as bad as I thought she might.

"I'll see Jim in heaven," she promised me. She thought without question, that when she left here, she was going to see her son. I'm still searching for such assurances in my own life.

We were all proud of Jim. When he'd retired from the navy as a rear admiral, another of Mother's dreams had come true.

I'm not the first man to discover that fathers and daughters are an extremely complex dynamic. My daughters, Lisa and Linda, are both strong-willed, independent women. I couldn't be prouder of them.

And yet, they tell me they wish I'd spent more time with them growing up. Maybe I could have taken them along when I was off hunting and fishing with the boys. This lapse bothers me a good bit. There's a hurt there, and maybe, like William Faulkner wrote, "The past is never dead. . . ."

Honestly, I never in my life thought that my girls would want to be out in the woods. I tell myself if only they'd asked ("Daddy why don't you take me?"), I'd have made an effort. Why wouldn't I? But there is another, deeper piece to it. I suspect Lisa and Linda, both fiercely talented and demanding children, weren't interested in trophy bass or a covey of quail exploding from the underbrush. They were pursuing me. And for them I was as elusive as my own father had been to me.

I *love* women, but I don't claim to understand them. I grew up in a masculine environment, and I've had a circle of male friends all the way back to high school and my days at UNC. The more the merrier. I still have a poker group; we play once a month and alternate from one person's house to the next. It's a dollar game. Maybe you lose $50, but you win companionship. One guy dies, and I bring another into the group. My daughter, Linda, thinks the fact that I'm able to "trade down" to younger and younger friends is what keeps me going. I don't know about that.

I can't explain these needs, and I've stopped trying. Ike Rolader was my best friend. We needed each other. My daughter, Lisa, says Ike was my real brother. I mentioned Dan Shepherd and the twice-a-day phone calls that went on for thirty years. It was never anything soul-searching, although we both had our challenges. Mostly we talked football or baseball—constant things in an inconstant world. As I've said already, Jimmy Barton, who went to North Fulton High with me, keeps an office right downstairs from mine. He's cantankerous as hell, but we go to lunch together once a week.

Like my father—and like many men of my generation—I have difficulty expressing my feelings. I'm not a hugger, and I don't compliment a lot. It's a fault. I know it, and I can appreciate the negative effect it has on others. I *do* react when something moves me, but I don't verbalize it. It's just not natural for me.

My circle of close friends would not be complete without Andrew Young. Andy, of course, is the renowned civil rights leader, former congressman, ambassador to the United Nations, and mayor of Atlanta. He is a great and courageous man whose life has been lived on the world stage.

Most friendships are based on familiarity. We befriend classmates, teammates, fraternity brothers, brothers-in-arms, colleagues, drinking buddies, and fellow carousers ("wild asses," in my case). Andy and I could not have been more different. He's a few years younger than I. His father was a dentist in New Orleans, while I grew up dirt-poor on Howell Mill Road. I was a street brawler; his daddy hired a pro boxer to teach Andy and his brother, Walter, the fine art of self-defense. He was called to the ministry; I was determined to make a million bucks in business.

Of course, much of this is beside the point. I'm white; Andy's black. We both grew up in the segregated South. The law declared I was the better man. It was always difficult for me—the eternal underdog—to stomach prejudice and segregation. So it was difficult to stand on the sidelines with the civil rights movement—in essence, a demand for justice, equal rights and *fairness*—swirling around me. I've described how Ike and I, in a scene right out of *Forrest Gump*, found ourselves in the middle of Martin Luther King Jr.'s historic march from Selma to Montgomery. Andy Young was there, but I didn't know him then. Yes, I went to check on my tents, but I saw a glimmer—how could I not?—of a cause much larger than myself.

Fifteen years would pass before we'd actually meet. By then, Aaron's was quite successful. I lunched at the Cherokee Country Club, lived in Buckhead, and was a part of the business establishment that has long dominated the city's power structure. As I've mentioned, prodded by leaders like Mills Lane and Mayors Bill Hartsfield and Ivan Allen, the business community grudgingly accepted that political power in Atlanta would inevitably flow to the African-American community. Maynard Jackson was elected mayor in 1973, the first black mayor of a major Southern city. But by 1980, many in the business community—myself included—felt that Jackson had divided the city along racial lines. It was time, the word in the corporate suites went, for a white candidate to take the reins of power.

Traditionally, businesses will donate money to the campaigns of both major candidates in a mayoral race. Although they certainly prefer one candidate over the other, they're covering their bets. When Maynard Jackson ran in 1972, my friend, Herman Russell, the well-known African-American developer, accompanied the candidate to my office and convinced me to donate $10,000 to the campaign. Herman was a fellow partner in the ownership of the Omni Arena and, like me, a part owner of the Atlanta Hawks and Atlanta Flames pro teams. For me that was a lot of money; it's a lot of money period. Well, Maynard won the election, but the next time I saw Maynard, he didn't speak to me. He also refused to speak at the all-white Atlanta Rotary Club. That's the kind of stuff he'd pull, and it irritated a lot of people.

Now it's 1980. Andrew Young announces his mayoral candidacy. I felt he had common sense, superlative credentials, and international notoriety, and he was hardly a polarizing figure. Early in the campaign, Andy showed up at my office, seeking my support. After our meeting, I walked him to the elevator. I told him I didn't know who I was going to support, but it would be whomever I felt could heal the divisions Mayor Jackson had exacerbated. A mayor who could put the city and the business community in sync again. Three or four days later, Andy shows up at my office. I'll let him pick up the story:

> *The business community had decided not to support another black mayor. They were really serious about needing somebody from their number as mayor. I went to Charlie and asked him if he'd break ranks with everybody else and work on my campaign. Honestly, I thought I could win the election without the business community, but I couldn't build a city with a split like that. Charlie and I agreed Atlanta could be a great city, but only if business and politics worked together, if blacks and whites worked together. No partisan politics, no racial politics. It was very important to Charlie to do what was fair. So, he became the co-chairman of my campaign.*

Risking his professional reputation, Charlie supported Andrew Young for mayor in 1980 to the great dismay of Atlanta's white business community.

That's the whole story in a nutshell. When I got home, I told Mickey and my kids, "Listen I'm going to support Andy Young. It's very controversial. You don't have to take any part in it, and you might even take some hell about it."

I found a vacant car dealership on Spring Street that would become Andy's campaign headquarters. Obviously the biggest part of my job was fund-raising. At the Rotary Club, I approached Bob Strickland, president and chairman of the Trust Company of Georgia (today, Sun Trust Banks). It was not only the most important bank in the state (Trust Company underwrote Coca-Cola's Initial Public Offering), but it's also my bank. I'd known Strickland for many years.

In fact, one of Andy's co-chairmen of his campaign, Jesse Hill, founder and CEO of the Atlanta

Life Insurance Company and a very prominent figure within and outside the African-American community, was on Trust Company's board. Strickland and I sat down outside the club.

"Bob," I said, "I'm going to support Andy Young for mayor, and I'd like you to get the bank's top guys together and let Andy come speak to you."

"No way!" Strickland shouts. "You cannot do that, Charlie!"

We went round and round. Finally, I said, "Bob, you know me. If I commit to something, I don't go back on it."

He wasn't too happy. Reluctantly, he agreed to invite Andy to address the senior staff at the bank.

Well, Andy showed up, and he gave the worst-received speech I've ever heard him give. The bankers wanted to hear what the next mayor would do about potholes, garbage collection, building up the police department. Andy talked about making Atlanta an "international city." He said his contacts from his days as UN ambassador would be a tremendous asset. Well, this kind of talk was over all our heads, including mine. Andy tried to explain that this status would be great for the business community. They had wanted to hear about crime, schools, and garbage services.

Afterward, I called Bob Strickland.

"Bob, what are you going to give Andy?"

"Nothing!" he shouted. "Absolutely nothing. Sidney Marcus is going to be the next mayor."

"Bob, I don't see it that way. It's going to be Andrew Young."

"Charlie, you may think you're the greatest political prognosticator, but I don't think you are."

Next, I called Ed Rast, president of Southern Bell. Ed was a forward-looking executive who invested in the computers and fiber optic technologies that helped transform Southern Bell from a phone company to a telecommunications giant.

"Over my dead body will Andrew Young be mayor of this city!" The man was apoplectic.

"I hope you're wrong," I managed. "I think Andy's going to be the next mayor, but I don't want you to die over it."

Dejected, I called Andy and Jesse Hill. We met in my office. "If my job is to get the white business community's support, I can't do it," I confessed. "We're not going to get any money to speak of because they're solidified behind [long-time state representative] Sidney Marcus." As best I could, I explained the business community wanted a white mayor. The racial divisions Maynard Jackson had exacerbated seemed to big to bridge.

They felt that Atlantans would elect Marcus mayor.

Silence.

After a moment, I blurted, "How much will it cost to run this campaign?"

Andy had no idea. He came up with a number—$300,000. I said, "Let me tell you: I'll guarantee the $300,000, but you've *got* to guarantee me you're not going to lose this damn election. If you do lose it, I'm going to have to move out of town! I'm out of here!" This was hardly an exaggeration. The bankers, the whole Buckhead bunch, were on my back.

We started raising money. Andy had to go out of town to New York, Los Angeles, and New Orleans to raise money from wealthy liberals. I borrowed the $300,000 from Sun Trust.

"What do you need it for?" the bankers looked at me suspiciously.

"To run Andy Young's campaign. I need a line of credit."

"We don't want to do that. We've had too much experience with political campaigns. If they lose, they can't pay. If they win, they don't want to pay. It's a bad deal."

"You don't understand. I'll *personally* guarantee it." That got their attention.

We spent close to $1 million on the campaign. In the last week of the race, I took a call from Stoney Cooks, Andy's operations manager.

Stoney wanted $10,000 in cash for an election day voter turnout drive. Volunteers manning the phone banks would make calls into the black community hoping to cherry-pick the last potential voters. The twist was to send taxis to pick up voters who couldn't get to the polls. At the time, this was a legal deal. Hell, I wasn't going to get $10,000 in an envelope from my bank and not say what it was for, or anything else. I called Herman Russell and went down to *his* bank—Citizen's Trust Bank—and gave them a check. Then I took $10,000 cash in a paper bag and gave it to Stoney. They lined up the cabs.

A few nights later, Andy Young became mayor of Atlanta.

The net of the whole thing was that Andy got 90 percent of the black vote. Sidney Marcus got 90 percent of the white vote. However, we got a huge voter turnout; they couldn't do the same among the whites. Andy, who puts a positive spin on everything, told me it wasn't a "racial vote."

"Andy, wait a minute," I said. "Any way you cut it, 90 percent is racial. Most elections swing on three or four percentage points. This one swung on 90 percent, both white and black."

On election night, Rev. Jesse Jackson showed up at the campaign headquarters. Andy's people wanted me in front of the TV cameras to emphasize that the victory reflected more than a racially divided electorate. Before I could speak, Jackson, never shy about publicity, shoved me completely away from the cameras and made sure he was standing next to Andy when the cameras rolled.

Well, Jackson's grandstanding—one of his trademarks—apparently made Jesse Hill, Herman Russell, Mack Wilbourn and the rest of Andy's local black supporters pretty mad. The next morning, Wilbourn, hosted a big victory breakfast at his house in Sherwood Forest. All of us had been up most of the night. They thanked me. All I said was, "We just elected the best person for the job."

They appreciated that. Of course, cynics in both the white and black communities were predicting I'd rush right down to City Hall and try to run things. In the heat of the campaign, Marcus's supporters, among them Joel Goldberg, former president of the Rich's department store chain, MARTA board member, and a big Sidney Marcus man, had allegedly been going around intimating my involvement in Andy's campaign had more to so with self-interest than good citizenship ("You know, Charlie Loudermilk doesn't do anything unless he makes money. He'll *own* City Hall and lease it back to the people.") I was learning quickly that politics is a rough and tumble business, which didn't seem all that different from life on Howell Mill Road.

At one point during the breakfast at Wilbourn's house, I took Andy off to the side.

"Now, I need to tell *you* what I want in return for all my efforts in your election."

Andy grew real quiet.

"Nothing! I'm closing the books on this event. Don't feel you have to call me. If I need to talk, I'll call you." And simply, that's the way it was. Over his tenure, Andy would drop by my office occasionally.

We'd talk about what folks on the Northside were thinking, that kind of stuff.

Andy later was quoted as saying, "Charlie paid quite a price for putting his short-term interests aside for the long-term good of the city." Well, considering what Andy accomplished, it wasn't much of a price, and it was short term. I'll take that deal any day.

Nobody burned any crosses on my lawn. As I said, the anger over my decision to support Andy came from my own peers and business associates. One memorable example occurred on the night that John Portman and I invited Andy and his wife Jean (since deceased) to the white tie Piedmont Ball at the Piedmont Driving Club. The event—the oldest of its kind in Atlanta—is a philanthropic bash linked to Piedmont Hospital and consistently draws sponsors from the city's social and business elite, and sponsors like the Ritz Carlton and Tiffany.

I pulled into the club on Piedmont Road, took a deep breath, and headed inside. By then, I'd long been a member and both my daughters had made their debuts there. Our table was right at the edge of the dance floor. We couldn't help but draw attention and more than a few frowns. I don't dance, but Mickey was a great dancer. She took a few turns around the dance floor with Andy Young. Later on, Mickey, who was wearing a black-and-white Oscar de la Renta gown, was approached by one of Buckhead's social butterflies.

"I'm glad you have on black and white," the woman sneered, "because you're half black and half white anyway!"

Mickey, always polite, smiled, but she was steaming. When we got home, she determined to exact her revenge. She decided to send the woman a bouquet of dead flowers, with, I assume, an appropriate message. I talked her out of it.

———

A few years after the election, Mayor Young contacted me. "Charlie, you know, this year, I appoint a new member to the MARTA board of directors," he began. MARTA is Atlanta's oft-troubled but vital mass transit system.

"That appointee will probably become chairman," Andy continued.

CITY OF ATLANTA

ANDREW YOUNG
MAYOR

Dec. 30, 1987

Dear Charlie,

Thanks very much for your continuing contributions to Atlanta and to me personally.

Our friendship and the trust that we share have done wonders for this city that no one will ever know about, and even if they knew, they wouldn't want to believe that "one" honest friendship could do so much to bind an entire city together.

The campaign, MARTA, now the Ga. Dome and God only knows what else might not have happened without your friendship. Thanks!

Have a great '88.

Peace and Blessings,

Andy

He went on to suggest that board member Joel Goldberg, the same fellow who'd allegedly trashed me during the mayoral campaign, wanted to be chairman, something Andy was not in favor of.

"Charlie, will you take the job?"

"Andy, let me think about it." I had never even ridden on a MARTA train. I finally said I'd do it.

When I got home, I told Mickey, "We've got to go ride the trains! We're going to ride east, west, north, and south. When the press asks me, I can tell them that I like this, that, and the other. This needs some improvement!"

Well, I spent four years on the MARTA board, two of them as chairman. It was no easy job, but I believe efficient, affordable mass transit is another one of those elements that is essential to a vibrant city. I approached MARTA with the same zeal with which I ran my business. A year after I became chairman, my secretary at Aaron's asked, "Do you know how many meetings you've had out of the office this year?"

"A lot?" I offered meekly.

"More than three hundred and most of them were for MARTA!"

There would be consequences for my leaving Aaron's unattended, but more on that later. I learned an awful lot during my MARTA stint. Frankly, at Aaron's I could call a meeting, sit at the table, and what I said was 100 percent. That was the end of it. I could tell my troops, "Run up the hill. If you get shot, you get shot."

The MARTA board was composed of rich and poor, male and female, young and old, black and white members; each had his or her own agenda and interests. The federal government, which had funded much of the system's initial cost, was looking over our shoulders, as was the state. There were real estate issues, safety concerns, and so many moving parts. To get anything done, you had to get the board with you. You had to build consensus. And I worked like hell to do it. All these years later, I still follow MARTA'S ups and downs, triumphs and crises. The biggest issue was getting the tracks up on the new Highway 400.

Over the years, Andy Young and I have remained friends. He was a great mayor and played a critical role in bringing the Olympics to Atlanta in 1996, the key, exactly as he predicted, to Atlanta joining the ranks of international cities. He brought the business community and the political leadership together for eight years until Maynard Jackson and Bill Campbell came back to city hall.

"I have no better friend in this world than Charlie Loudermilk," Andy Young said at a 2009 address to the Rotary Club. I feel the same way about Andrew.

He's a black, liberal Democrat. I'm a white, conservative Republican. We value each other's friendship and opinions, but we don't always agree. Andy feels he has the right to express his opinion and that I have the right to express mine. That's very important in today's chaotic world. Respect the person who's giving the opinion even though you don't agree with it. Isn't that the essence of friendship?

I began this chapter talking about the importance of family and friends. Other than my brother Jim's tragic death, my family has been so fortunate. Mother lived to be ninety-six years old. She appreciated my successes, but to her dying day she remained convinced that I was going to lose everything I'd earned. My three kids are great; my five grandchildren are just *phenomenal*. Robin and I constantly try to imbue our business with Mother's work ethic, values, caring nature, and family sensibility. That's our ultimate goal. Her last years were happy because she felt that she accomplished her goal of raising two successful boys.

Children and grandchildren are now Charlie's priority—family and friends are what matter most to him.

Charlie beams while talking about his daughter Linda (left), and her many successes as a talented, eco-friendly fashion designer living in Los Angeles.

Charlie's son Robin and his family (opposite) share Charlie's love for the outdoors. Left to right: Robin, Chappell, Frances, and Charlie hold the youngest in their family, daughter Coley.

Charlie is extremely proud of his daughter Lisa who with her interior design expertise has assisted her father in his business as well as in other joint endeavors. Left to right: Michael, Robert, Lisa, and Katharine.

Chapter Fourteen

*"The success or failure of any business is to a large degree
the responsibility of the top guy."*
— Charlie Loudermilk on Aaron's near-bankruptcy

I took Aaron's public in 1982. In a perfect world, all the sweat and tears we'd expended over the first twenty-seven years building the company would be rewarded, and the endless and frustrating quest for capital to grow the business, satisfied. Only a year later, we were operating ninety-two stores in fourteen states, up from three Atlanta-based outlets in 1963. In 1983, our sales topped $55 million, the rental industry was booming, and visions of enduring entrepreneurial glory shimmered before my eyes.

Before I go on, here's a bit of background you won't find in the annual reports. A few years earlier, I'd lined up a small group of investors to help fund my move into the furniture rental business. At the time, we were operating as two separate entities, a party and a sick room supply rental company and a separate furniture rental company, the predecessors to Aaron's. A share sold for $5,000 and, in total, I raised about $95,000. Ike Rolader put up $25,000. Robert Corr, another dentist, invested $35,000. Some of the others partners were Frank and Crawford Sikes, Gene Caverly, my attorney Tom Shelton, Jack Wall, and the Kilpatrick law firm.

We all decided we needed to merge the two companies. Robert Corr strongly disagreed, insisting his investment was intended only to fund the furniture rental operation. As I recall, he had a brother, maybe a vice president of the Greyhound bus line, who was advising him. Our accountants and lawyers all said it was a fair deal. Well, Corr sued us, and the case eventually went to trial in Fulton County Superior Court.

The judge advised the lawyers on both sides not to get too technical. The statutes governing mergers and acquisitions would appear pretty arcane to the average juror. In any event, the jury ruled against us. Two hours after the decision, I was sitting at home commiserating, when the phone rang. It was the foreman from the jury, a woman who owned a small furniture store.

"This was an injustice!" the woman exclaimed. "After a few hours of deliberations, the other jurors were screaming and hollering that they wanted to go home. I couldn't do anything about it...."

That's a story anyone who has had any dealing with the courts has heard before. It's a shame that a trial by a jury of one's peers, the absolute essence of a fair and just society, can be taken so lightly. She suggested I appeal the verdict.

Our lawyer, Barry Phillips, at Kilpatrick filed an appeal and the process dragged on for seven years. When it was finally over, Dr. Corr was awarded only his original investment—$35,000—no interest, nothing. When we went public, the other investors reaped $1 million for each $5,000 they'd put in. Corr's lawsuit wound up costing him $7 million.

Another investor, Frank Owens, sold off his share prematurely because his wife insisted he use the $5,000 to build an addition to their home. Many years later, I met the man's son-in-law at a golf tournament. He told me the story had become a family legend. His father-in-law was still grumping about his "million-dollar room." Ike Rolader used one of his millions to buy a divorce.

Just a few years after the initial public offering, I found myself in a desperate struggle to keep the company afloat. My mother's fears about my going bust were suddenly very plausible. In short, Aaron's ran into a perfect storm and no one was at the tiller.

I should have seen the warning signs. Our steady growth through the sixties, seventies, and early eighties was fueled, in part, by demographics. A great in-migration of jobs, capital, and population into Atlanta and other Sunbelt states spurred the furniture rental business, both residential and corporate. In 1982, I sold off our party and sick room equipment rental operations and used the proceeds to buy furniture. As I've mentioned, setting up our own furniture-manufacturing operations—MacTavish—put us at a tremendous advantage over our competitors in terms of cost and speed to market. Tax laws, particularly our ability to quickly depreciate and write-off inventory, were very favorable.

Our business strategy demands aggressive growth and expansion. Funded by our 1982, initial public offering, we went into acquisition mode, buying up competitors such as Metrolease and Modern Furniture Rental. Our stores were bigger and better stocked than those of tough competitors like Grantree and Rent-A-Center. By 1984, we were the largest private furniture rental company in the country with annual revenues of $84 million.

In early 1986, we were operating 150 stores in twenty states, and Aaron's revenue—a good bit of it fueled by acquisitions—surged toward $100 million. Profits, however, do not march in lockstep with revenue growth. Each new store, for example, required between a year and eighteen months to move into the black. Long-term success is dependent on a number of variables, separate and apart from the inevitable swings of the business cycle. I'm talking about the impact of leadership on employee morale and performance, knowledge as opposed to raw information, and most importantly, the vibrant, respectful, day-to-day connection that must be forged between a service business and the consumer.

While I served on the MARTA board and a dozen or so civic or community projects, Aaron's continued to make money, but sales began outpacing earnings, a warning sign I was too busy to take heed of. Without getting too technical, we were growing faster—opening more and more stores and acquiring other companies—than we could swallow. Some of our success was on paper. For example, the Tax Reform Act of 1986 boosted profitability (corporate tax rates dropped from 46 to 34 percent) but was offset by the loss of many of our depreciation benefits. The furniture rental, a rent-to-rent business, was slowing down. A new model—rent-to-own—was beginning to transform the industry. We were a little slow off the mark. The bottom line: our stock fell from a high of $25 in 1984 to $12 in the summer of 1987. And the crash of 1987 was just a few months away. The stock eventually bottomed out at $6.

My daughters mentioned that I was part of a group that built the Omni Complex and owned the Atlanta Hawks and Flames (predecessor to the NHL Thrashers). I was. I was also fortunate to be able to engage in community service and philanthropic outreaches at UNC, the Atlanta Community Food Bank, Lovett School, Piedmont Hospital Foundation, and others. These are ties I maintain to this day.

I also bought myself a toy, a 5,000-acre spread, Woodhaven Plantation, in Coolidge, Georgia. In essence, "Jeep" Loudermilk went from raising a skinny calf in the backyards to breeding herds of Limousin cattle. I was a quail hunter, a dove hunter, and a fox hunter on horseback.

My marriage was wobbling badly.

Charlie's beloved recreational retreat is a 5,000-acre spread called Woodhaven Plantation in Coolidge, Georgia. Coolidge is also the home of one of Aaron's furniture manufacturing plants which has helped him provide opportunity, employment, and recreation to a grateful community.

In short, I was bored. I'd made an executive decision to appoint presidents for each of Aaron's divisions from within the ranks. Essentially, I'd walked away. In retrospect, it was not something a focused and committed chief executive would have done. Aaron's was my baby. I'd poured more into her than I had poured into my own family. Would Mother—by the way, at that point she'd turned all her stock over to me—have considered walking away from her restaurants?

Effectively abdicating control of the company was a disaster, something out of *King Lear*. My presidents—executives I'd known for years—started fighting among themselves. They built fiefdoms and walls around their areas of responsibility. Aaron's went from a vertical organization with me at the top of the chain of command, to a malfunctioning horizontal operation, to chaos. No one was communicating with anyone else, and I was off worrying about MARTA schedules and fare increases. Profits declined; investor confidence plummeted. By the end of 1987, our stock was hovering around $6.50 a share. I remember going to lunch with my chief financial officer, a guy I trusted. We stared at each other until one of us said,

"What the hell is going on?"

How worried was I at that point? I resigned from MARTA and most other civic commitments. I told my children to dump $300,000 in stock I'd given them.

Fortunately, rather than a death knell, it was a wake-up call. I came back, took day-to-day control of the company, cut back our stores from 180 to 130 to get my hands around the business. I had to push my top executives out to put the company back together again. It wasn't easy or quick. If you have any heart, you don't like to fire anyone. You start thinking about families and kids. I told myself they'd fired themselves. They wouldn't run the business the way it should have been run. I told myself they should have known how to run it. Didn't they learn it from me? But that wasn't true either.

What is true, what my mother taught me and I should never have lost sight of, is that the success or failure of any company is to a large degree the responsibility of the top guy. If the top guy is stealing or sleeping or drunk—including drunk on his own ego—everybody is stealing and sleeping and drunk.

We turned the company around. Strategically, we moved into the rent-to-own model, which remains our bread-and-butter business today. A franchising campaign increased our regional coverage with minimal capital outlay. These moves, it's fair to say, laid the groundwork for our future success. Notwithstanding, Aaron's suffered three more years of declining sales and earnings (1989–1991). I'll let Gil Danielson, today Aaron's chief financial officer, tell a very short version of the story. He's taken a closer look at how it unfolded. I try to avoid the 20/20 benefits of hindsight:

When Charlie came back, he got into it, in detail. Seven days a week, twenty-four-hours a day, he gathered information, got very close to the stores, talked to everybody. Observed everything. Aaron's was his baby; he'd started it. Of course, he had a lot of knowledge, but it was the ability to grab hold of it, and using his instincts and his knowledge and his desire and competitiveness, he wrenched it back on track. He's the owner. The guys who were running the thing were employees. That's a whole different mentality.

I do remember getting all our managers into a room. I believed if I provided the leadership most of them would follow. Not all, however, did. Honestly, some were in the wrong business. Everybody is put together differently. A lot of people would not have a job if they couldn't close the books at five o'clock. Today, I say this to men and women trying to get into this business, "You never, ever have an hour that you don't have something to do in a rental store. And when you do leave, you leave with a lot on your brain that you're going to bring back into the morning."

If the customers see you're not around to collect, they won't pay. They've got too many other pressing demands on their money. As for a manager, if you can't make the numbers work, top and bottom line, change careers. Become a fireman, policeman, or whatever; running a store is not for you. A lot of times, they don't want to admit it. They don't want to give up because there's a lot of money to be made. Eventually, they quit because they can't keep up the pace. There's no shame in that. Ken Butler came up with the phrase that sums it all up: "You are what your numbers say you are."

"Tell me what you're going to do?" I demanded of the group. "What are you going to do?" I pointed to one person, then another. The responses started building, and some of the ideas made good sense. I could feel the energy building.

"We're going to do this! We're going to do that!"

"We'll do it!" a woman shouted.

"We're gonna turn it around!"

And we did. Was this so different from my college days at UNC, running for this or that office, rousing my constituencies? Was it different from the tent revivals that used to blow into Atlanta when I was a boy aware of the spirit rising from the sawdust floors?

Throughout my career, I've stressed *fairness* as a guiding principal. I believe there is no brighter star in the heavens to guide a state, a life, a company, a career. At Aaron's, we've always been aware of the predators in our industry, and we determined long ago that we would never treat our customers and our employees as numbers to be squeezed and manipulated on a balance sheet. What I'm saying is, a used car salesman will not be happy at Aaron's. We *do not* tolerate lying to our customers or employees.

I'm hardly exceptional in these beliefs, but I can say that as a boy in working-class Atlanta, what I wanted most was a chance, a level playing field, and an honest shot. Give me that, and you give me dignity. I'll take it the rest of the way. Many of Aaron's 1.7 million customers are not so different from my own childhood family. The easy phrase is that they are "credit-challenged," but the truth is they want a scrap of dignity, whether it's a computer, a living room suite, or maybe a set of well-made twin beds for their kids. I still remember my mother's thrill at being able to purchase "on time" that long ago pair of mahogany beds for Jim and me.

Many of Aaron's customers have been buffeted, for whatever reasons, by life and are trying to move forward. We don't check their credit or string out their payments. We give them their shot at ownership. And it's a shot, by the way, that most won't get at Wal-Mart. Many prove as good as their word in living up to their commitments.

I'm not big on psychological analysis, but I guess the boy who didn't have shoes to wear to the Fritz Orr Camp is still alive somewhere inside of me. That boy was given a chance. That child is father to the man.

A company always takes on the personality of its leadership. Last year, my son, Robin, became Aaron's CEO, a leader of great heart and compassion.

Our employees are Aaron's greatest asset. Transmitters of our culture. The hope for our future. A few years back, we suffered a terrible loss. Three women working at one of our plants were struck by a truck. All were killed. Word gets around quickly, and it came to my attention that the director of a funeral home in Moultrie was demanding what seemed to be an extortionate fee to bury them. By then, he'd held up the funeral for more than a week. I called the funeral home and spoke to the man. I was furious when he confirmed the cost. It was unfair.

"That's way too much money!"

We went round and round.

"Tell you what I'll do," I finally said. "I'll write you a check right now for x dollars. I'll mail it today. You bury these people. Give them a great funeral."

And he did. We do things like this all the time. It's not something we publicize. Was it unseemly for the CEO of a major company to be haggling over the cost of a funeral? I don't think so. Aaron's paid a funeral expense, but a message went out to thousands of our employees and franchisees: "You are our family. We'll always be there for you."

Two years ago, I was visiting our store in Brunswick, Georgia. I was standing next to our manager who was talking to a customer on the phone. The customer didn't have enough money to pay the rent on her computer so he asked her to pay half then and pay the balance on her next pay day. I asked him what the rent was and noticed on the contract that it was a used computer.

"Why are you charging this lady the cost of a new computer?" I asked.

He explained that when she rented the computer he did not have a new one in stock. She told him she would be happy to rent the used one until a new computer came in. When the new one arrived, she said that she wanted to keep the computer she had been using. I told him to call and tell her the rental price for her used computer and that we will refund the difference before she makes another payment. I had forgotten about that incident until recently, but the store manager has told that story many times to other employees.

What did I learn from all these years in business? I'd like to say I'm all things to all people . . . that I've finally established an easy balance between my personal life and the demands of my career. It wouldn't be true. Honestly, I've tried. People don't understand that you don't make the success in business that I made without being direct and straight to the bottom line. You can make a lot a lot of mistakes by getting too emotional. Has this spilled over into my family life? Of course, it has.

Opposite: Charlie and his son Robin together guide Aaron's to even bigger things, ever ready for the next big adventure.

CHAPTER FIFTEEN

*"If I'd talked to her for two minutes every day, it would have given her such joy.
I never hugged her. I think she missed that her whole life. Some people
think I'm a saint because I kept her in a big house next to the
governor's mansion. She deserved the biggest house in Atlanta."*

—CHARLIE LOUDERMILK ON ADDIE'S LAST YEARS

Mother's legs finally gave out. All those years on her feet, all those thousands of miles walked in her restaurants taking their toll. I can still see her bustling around the Fritz Orr Camp . . . imagine her pushing Jim and me up the hill on Howell Mill Road in our baby carriages, carrying us relentlessly toward a better life, a fierce angel driven by pure energy and unconditional love. The sacrifices she made day-in and day-out, getting up at dawn and going to work, working late into the night, grabbing a few hours of sleep and starting over again. I don't know anyone who paid that kind of price and took so little in return. She was a doer. My mother did what she wanted to do.

And she was not unhappy doing it.

She would live for the better part of a century and see things—two world wars, men walking on the moon, an Atlanta Olympics—beyond imagining. She would watch the family she birthed blossom and thrive over three generations. She'd lose a son and see another build a thriving business with his own hands, hands she'd scrubbed when I was a boy. I would like to believe she saw part of herself in me because whatever I've done or achieved I trace directly back to her example and inspiration. I made her my business partner; she laughed and turned all her stock over to me, never took a nickel.

After my father passed, I moved Mother out of the small apartment on Roswell Road, to a house on Woodhaven Road next to the governor's mansion close to where I lived. In fact, the mansion's fence

Opposite: Charlie's mother Addie enjoying a visit at Woodhaven Plantation.

was her backyard. By now, I was pretty well known around town. Over the years, the governors' wives—Elizabeth Harris, Mary Beth Busbee, and Shirley Miller—kind of adopted her as their mother and would invite her up to the mansion events and give her Christmas and Mothers' Day presents. She got a big kick out of that. To be raised blue collar and wind up living next to the governor's mansion was big thing. To go up there and be in that house, what a thrill for her.

By then, she'd had both her knees replaced. She didn't do the physical therapy, and her legs atrophied. Aging and confined to a wheelchair, she was subject to all the insults and indignities of old age, many of which I'm starting to feel myself. Her mind, however, remained clear as a bell, as did that uncanny sixth sense that alerts mothers when loved ones are troubled or threatened.

One day, out of the blue, she asked me, "What's wrong with Lisa?"

"What do you mean what's wrong?" I replied. "What are you talking about? You haven't even seen Lisa in a while."

"Charlie, she just doesn't sound right."

Of course Mother was right. My daughter was struggling with some personal issues. And I'd missed it completely.

A long driveway wound up to the Woodhaven Road house. The house was laid out all on one level, so Mother could get right out of a car and into her wheelchair. I had at least one lady staying with her twenty-four hours a day for more than a decade. I put Becky Copeland, a dear woman who still babysits for my daughter, in charge of these caregivers.

Mother insisted she wouldn't take a new car from me. I bought her one anyway, a Cadillac. She was upset with the expense—she still figured I was on the road to financial ruin. At first, she told me she didn't like it, but after two or three weeks, she smiled at me.

"Charlie, I like that car!"

One of the ladies would drive her around town. Once a week or so, she'd come by my office on East Paces Ferry Road. She and Becky would ride the elevator to the eleventh floor to pick up the payroll checks for the other ladies or sometimes just to visit. The phones would be jangling, and I'd be running around busy . . . busy . . . busy. My secretary, Pam Black, would give them the checks. Don't you know; I didn't take the time to sit down and talk to her. Never reached over and hugged her. Even today, people praise me for the wonderful care I provided. They don't know that emotionally, I really wasn't there. I wasn't doing the job for her.

You see, I lived just two blocks from Woodhaven Road, and every day I'd drive by her house going and coming from work. In the mornings, I'd be in a big rush; in the evenings it'd be so late, I'd tell myself, "I've got to get home and get to bed. I'll see her tomorrow. Tomorrow there'll be time." And a week would pass.

I ought to have stopped by. Even if we'd talked for just a few minutes, it would have given her such joy. Lord knows, I should have hugged her. I think she missed that her whole life. Sometimes, I can feel my arms reaching out to her, but she's not there and will never be again in this life. She loved me unbelievably. I should have poured out all the things I've struggled to get down on these pages. Instead, it was she who bragged to everyone what a great son her Charlie was. They thought I was a saint because I kept her in that big, empty house.

I was at work when she died. The call came into the office around 9:00 A.M. on Tuesday, October 29, 1996. I rushed over to the house on Woodhaven. Becky Copeland was not on duty that day; another woman was caring for Mother. The lady was scared, in a near-panic. I stood stunned, wracked by grief, trying to comprehend what she was saying.

"Your mother was very upset last night," the woman blurted. "I gave her twice as much medication to calm her down."

Twice as much medication! Later, when I talked her doctor who told me all Mother's vital organs were in good shape. He listed the cause of death as cerebral infarction, a stroke, and then added, "I don't understand what killed her."

I believe I do. But I can't bring her back, and I wasn't about to sue the woman. As it turned out, she was neither a nurse or healthcare professional. She had no idea what she'd done. And there was nothing I could do about it. Mother was ninety-six years old. She'd lived a very full life. She was a woman of faith. I'm sure she was prepared to stand before God. I was the one who felt empty. There was a hole in my heart that, for all my success and the best efforts of a loving family, remains unfilled to this day.

Two days before she died, she looked me straight in the eye—keep in mind I was in my late sixties but I was still her baby—and, sure enough, she said "Charlie, are you going broke?"

"Mother," I said, "I've got millions."

She laughed.

Her memorial service was held at the Rock Spring Presbyterian Church on Piedmont Road, a house of worship she'd loved since she was a girl living up the road in shotgun shack that the railroad offered as housing to her father. I met with the pastor and explained to him that my children wanted to speak about their grandmother at the service. To my outrage, he argued that they shouldn't. I guess he was determined to be the center of attention at what he imagined to be a rich lady's funeral. (I heard he allegedly left the congregation after some impropriety a year later.) In any event, my children wanted to speak, and they did. I'm so proud of them for that.

Today, if you visit the Rock Spring church you find the Addie Loudermilk Hall, a building I donated that is used as a recreation center. Mother would surely have enjoyed the children giggling and running around in the after-school program. It was the least I could do.

Mother is buried next to my father in Arlington Memorial Park, a Sandy Springs cemetery not far

from where the two of them lived and finally grew close in their later years. Believe me, going to graves, visiting children's hospitals, or stopping to see the grievously injured young men and women at the Shepherd Center is not something I can easily do. I don't trust myself. I'm afraid I'll lose control, let my emotions get the best of me. But my conscience bothers me about not doing these things. I've said many times, "Judge me by my actions, not whether I wear my emotions on my sleeve for everyone to see."

Sometimes, I have a very hard time taking my own advice. Other times, I feel beaten down and uncertain. When I do, when I feel the old insecurities and inferiority complexes rising in me like bile, and when I feel the pull of so many unfinished tasks dragging me down, I remind myself of Mother's enduring words, blessings sprung from her heart like gentle rain in springtime:

"Charlie, just do better next time."

And I am not afraid. I know she is with me.

Timeline

1943 Charlie Loudermilk graduates from North Fulton High School and enrolls at Georgia Tech.
1945 Charlie enlists in the U.S. Navy.
1950
- Charlie graduates from UNC with a Bachelor of Science degree in Business Administration.
- Charlie is hired as a salesman for Charles Pfizer and Company.

Early- to mid-1950s
- Charlie and his mother Addie open a restaurant, The Rose Bowl II, as they continue to run Addie's first restaurant, a successful tea room in Atlanta called The Rose Bowl.
- Addie and Charlie open a third restaurant, The Rose Bowl III, in the Cox-Carlton Hotel across from the Fox Theater in Atlanta.

1955 Charlie and a partner found Aaron Rents, Inc. 300 chairs are rented for 10 cents per day.
1965 Aaron Rents provides four tents for the civil rights march from Selma to Montgomery, Alabama.
1967 Aaron's opens its first store outside of Atlanta, in Baltimore, Maryland.
1970 Charlie becomes involved with Big Brothers Big Sisters of Metro Atlanta.
1971 Aaron Rents begins to manufacture furniture in a newly acquired plant.
1974 Ken Butler joins Aaron's (and works there still).
1981 Charlie is co-chairman of Andrew Young's Atlanta Mayoral campaign.
1982
- Initial public offering of company stock.
- Furniture manufacturing operations begin in Coolidge, Georgia. Many jobs are provided to the community as well as new housing, a recreation center, a lighted baseball field, and the implementation of a sewage system.

1985 Charlie is co-chairman of Andrew Young's Atlanta Mayoral re-election campaign.
1986 Aaron's annual revenues pass $100,000,000.
1987
- The rent-to-own concept, the predecessor of the sales and lease ownership program is introduced by Aaron Rents.
- Charlie serves as chairman of the Omni Group that builds the Omni and owns the Atlanta Flames and Hawks.

1987 First cash dividend.
1989 Charlie builds Woodhaven Plantation on 5,000 acres in Coolidge, Georgia.
1992 First franchised store is awarded and opens.
1994
- Secondary offering of 1.3 million company shares raises $14 million.
- Charlie serves on the board of directors of the Corporation for Olympic Development and Executive Committee of the Atlanta Convention and Visitors Bureau Board of Directors, 1996 Olympics.
- Charlie is a member of the board of Lovett School, Morris Brown College, and Piedmont College.
- Charlie is chairman of the board of directors for Metropolitan Atlanta Rapid Transit Authority (MARTA).

1996
- Death of Addie Loudermilk, mother and early business partner of Charlie Loudermilk.

- Charlie conceives of the idea to use the facade from the 1901 Carengie Central Library in Atlanta (long ago demolished) to create a pavilion as a monument to higher education. Along with the Corporation for Olympic Development in Atlanta (CODA), he helps fund the Carnegie Education Pavilion and locate it to Hardy Ivy Park.

1997
- Charlie is cofounder and chairman of the board of The Buckhead Community Bank.
- Charlie is founder of the Buckhead Coalition, which serves on behalf of the community of Buckhead.

1998
- Aaron's stock is listed on the NYSE.
- Secondary offering of 2.1 million shares raises $40 million.

1999 Charlie is co-chairman of Atlanta Action Forum, a group of 20 white and 20 African-American successful professionals who come together in an effort to involve the African-American community in community issues and changes.

2000
- Aaron's acquires 82 locations from Heilig-Meyers.
- Aaron's opens its 500th store.
- Charlie is awarded The Armin Maier Award in recognition of his unselfish service to his city, for his ideals and performance in good citizenship, and for his exemplary fidelity to the principles and objectives of Rotary International.
- Charlie is awarded The William Richardson "Davie Award" by the Board of Trustees of UNC at Chapel Hill.
- Charlie joins forces with the United Way of Metro Atlanta to open the Loudermilk Center, to meet the needs of civic-minded businesses and organizations.

2002
- Secondary offering of 1.7 million shares raises $34 million.
- Charlie funds a 123,000 square foot Upper School Loudermilk Student Activities Center housing a faculty resource center, a café, and a gymnasium with a suspended track.
- Charlie donates $1 million for a new organ at Peachtree Road Methodist Church.

2003
- Total company and franchised store revenues exceed $1 billion.
- Charlie funds the construction of a new stadium at Piedmont College in honor of his grandparents, Henry and Beulah Loudermilk.
- Charlie funds the Loudermilk Building in downtown Atlanta in support of the United Way.
- Charlie serves on the Piedmont Hospital Foundation Board, the Atlanta Community Food Bank, and the Archbold Hospital Foundation in Thomasville, Georgia.
- Charlie funds and develops Jacob's Ladder, an 18-acre property that provides homes for children who have none or live in dangerous or difficult conditions.
- First Aaron Rents stores are opened by franchisee in Canada.

2004 Aaron's moves from semiannual to quarterly cash dividends, payout is doubled.

2005
- Aaron Rents celebrates its 50th anniversary.
- Groundbreaking for the 1,000th Aaron's store.
- Annual revenues pass $1 billion.
- Charlie serves on the board of visitors for the University of North Carolina School of Business.
- Charlie donates $1.5 million to the Andrew Young Park and statue in Atlanta.
- Charlie donates $3 million to fund a new cardiac and vascular treatment center named R. Charles Loudermilk, Sr. Heart and Vascular Center, in Thomasville, Georgia.

2007 Charlie receives an Honorary Doctorate of Economics from Georgia State University.

2008
- Charlie Loudermilk's son Robin takes over

Aaron Rents as CEO.

- A Warren Buffett company buys Aaron Rents corporate furnishings division.
- Charlie is awarded Association of Progressive Rental Organization's 2008 Lifetime Achievement Award.
- Charlie is awarded the *Business to Business* 2008 Philanthropist of the Year Award.
- Charlie is awarded the Boisfeuillet Jones Award for a life of business and community leadership. He then donates $10,000 to the other 10 recipients to support their volunteer work.
- The Atlanta City Council votes to change the name of Buckhead Triangle Park to Charlie Loudermilk Park.
- Charlie is inducted into the Junior Achievement of Georgia Hall of Fame where he then pledges $500,000 to support its K–12 "Economics of Life" program across Georgia.
- Charlie is appointed by Governor Sonny Purdue as a member of the Georgia Music Hall of Fame.

2009
- Charlie is awarded the Lifetime Achievement Award by the Georgia Rental Dealers Association.
- Charlie is awarded the Marion Collier Ross Leadership Award by the Rotary Club of Atlanta.
- Aaron Rents, Inc. changes its name to Aaron's, Inc. which has grown to 1,675+ stores.

2010
- Aaron's is awarded the *Business to Business* Company of the Year Award.
- Charlie partners with Alex Cooley to purchase The Roxy and restore it with its original name The Buckhead Theatre, a Spanish Baroque movie house built in 1927.

"I get a helluva lot more out of it than I put into it.
I know that sounds Pollyannaish, but I just do. I like the feeling
that I am contributing and impacting the lives of people."

—CHARLIE LOUDERMILK